God Almighty!

HIS WORD
for Christians, Jews, and Moslems

William

Lester Fleenor

CROSE

T5-AFS-699

In Appreciation

For
the following women and men
(among many others)
who have had a profound impact on my life:

Monda, Kay, Irene, and Ann;
S. Joseph, J. Kilmer, G. Newberry,
G. Kufeldt, J. Massey, D. McCarty,
P. Matheney, and J. Howell.

Copyright © 2005 by Lester Fleenor

For ordering information contact Evangel Press. 1-800-253-9315

ISBN: 1-928915-67-1

Library of Congress Catalog Card Number: 2005926034

Dedication

To the martyrs and those imprisoned and persecuted for the sake of following the One True God, and to their suffering families, I dedicate this book. Also, to those courageous searchers after God in every nation, tribe, and language who have found the way, the truth, and the life; among them my close friends, Richard and Ahmed.

In addition, I dedicate this book to the messengers scattered throughout the world who are on the front lines risking their lives for the goal of leading others to find their God-intended destiny.

Foreword

*T*hose of us who travel, work, and/or live among persons from other cultures, languages, and backgrounds quickly notice the differences and similarities from our own. In getting acquainted with new friends and sharing in terms of religious beliefs, we are often faced with the same identity question which Moses expressed to God:

> "If I go to the people...and tell them that their fathers' God has sent me, they will ask, 'Which God are you talking about?' What shall I tell them?"
>
> Exodus 3:13, *The Living Bible*

This book is my attempt to answer this "Which God?" question by looking at three aspects: God's name, the concept of His power and greatness, and the manner in which He has revealed Himself to man. The focus is on the three world religions (Judaism, Christianity, and Islam) that I am closely acquainted with and which are unified in believing in only one God, and in boldly declaring that His nature is one of inconceivable power, authority, and majesty. Any one name is insufficient for man to describe Him and evidence of this can be seen in Islam's attempt to give Him ninety-nine names, and in the fact that the Jewish and Christian scriptures contain many names that even God, Himself, gave His followers in order to widen their understanding.

Since names and concepts can only go so far, God has expanded revelation about Himself through His acts and relationships with man throughout history. The reader is encouraged to initiate a personal encounter with God just as Moses' people personally experienced His providential presence and deliverance starting with their frightening experience of escape from slavery in Egypt. May God Almighty give all honest seekers courage to start this journey with the confidence that He will be guiding each step of the way through the hard places in the desert with the promise that their thirst will ultimately be quenched.

Word Clarifications

Names for the one true God:
Arabic language - Allah, Ilah, Allahum
Aramaic language - Elah, Alaha
Hebrew language - El, Eloah, Elohim, Allahu, Yahweh, among others

Names for the Messiah (Christ):
Arabic language - alMasih
Aramaic language - alMesiha
Hebrew language - haMoshiach
Greek language - Christos

Names for Jesus:
Arabic language - Yasua (used by Christians) and Isa (used by Moslems)
Aramaic language - Yesu
Hebrew language - Y'shua

The word "Almighty" or "Greatest" (referring to God):
Arabic language - Akbar
Hebrew language - Kabeer or Kabbir, Shaday or Shadai

Main Religious Writings or Scriptures:

Islam – Quran, Hadith

Judaism – Torah, Prophets, Writings

Christianity – The Bible (Old and New Testaments)

Quran – The book of religious teachings which the prophet of Islam claimed to have received in the Arabic language directly from God (Allah) through the angel Gabriel. Changes are noted in the modern English language translations of the Quran from the older translations and the original Arabic text. Some explain this to be a result of the current attempt to soften the meaning for the western reader. Therefore the person reading the Quran in English will find some differences from the original Arabic. Whenever possible, refer to a close translation of the original Arabic words and meanings.

Hadith – A compilation of the sayings of the prophet of Islam.

Torah – The first five books of the Old Testament, sometimes called the "Law of Moses."

Jihad – the term from the Quran meaning "to struggle" or "to strive;" sometimes used to describe spiritually struggling for faith and Islamic evangelism, but more commonly used to mean fighting on behalf of Allah in a "holy war."

Muslim or Moslem – a person who submits to Allah of Islam.

"In the thirtieth year, ... while I was among the exiles ..., the heavens were opened and I saw visions of **God**. ... Spread out above the heads of the living creatures was what looked like an expanse, sparkling like ice, and awesome. When the (living) creatures moved, I heard the sound of their wings, ... like the voice of the Almighty. ... Above their heads was ... a throne of sapphire ... and on the throne was a figure like that of a **man**. ... Like the appearance of a **rainbow** in the clouds on a rainy day, so was the radiance around him. This was the appearance of the likeness of the glory of the Lord."

(Ezekiel 1:1, 22, 24, 26, 28)

Table of Contents

PART I

God and Allah: the Same or Different?

Is "Allah" An Arabic Name for the Triune God?

*Y*es, Allah is the name of the true God for the Christian Arabs. Are you shocked?...Please wait!

In my experiences throughout the Middle East, I have never met, as I have in Africa and North and South America, anyone who believes in any other than the one, all powerful, creator God. Also, in the Middle East where over 20,000,000 Christians live, I have yet to hear any one of them, while speaking or praying in Arabic, use a different name for God instead of *Allah*. Many Westerners argue that the name Allah can by no means be used to refer to the God of Christians and Jews. Some Western writers say that this name was the name of the pagan moon god in southern Arabia before it was adopted by Islam. In fact, however, Allah was the original name that Arabic speaking Jews and Christians had for the God of Abraham, Isaac, Jacob, Moses, David, and yes...Jesus.

The *Oxford Encyclopedia of the Modern Islamic World* says that the name "Allah (a contraction of al-ilah), is the same God worshiped, to the exclusion of all others, by Jews and Christians." [1]

The name Allah has its background in the Semitic languages of the Middle East. It is an Arabic contraction of the definite

2

article al- and the usual word for deity 'ilah, (al-ilah) making Allah which means "the God." Ilah is the general term for God in the Arabic language equivalent to the Hebrew Eloah (singular) and Elohim (plural), and the Aramaic Elah or Alaha.[2] The *World Christian Encyclopedia's* list of names for God (originally based on a listing prepared by the British and Foreign Bible Society) used in translations of the Scriptures in some nine hundred languages showed two names in the Hebrew language: *Allahu* and *Elohim*,[3] while the only name used for God in the Arabic language was *Allah*.[4]

Vine's Expository Dictionary says: "this ('elah, 'god') Aramaic word is the equivalent of the Hebrew 'eloah. It is a general term for 'God' in the Aramaic passages of the Old Testament, and it is a cognate of the word Allah, the designation of deity used by the Arabs. The word was used widely in the Book of Ezra, occurring no fewer than 43 times between Ezra 4:24 and 7:26. On each occasion, the reference is to the 'God' of the Jewish people, whether the speaker or writer was himself Jewish or not."[5]

One for all and all for ONE!

Jesus' plea on the cross to His Father is still preserved in our Bibles in His native tongue, Aramaic: "Eloi, Eloi (Elahi, Elahi), lama sabachthani?" ("My God, my God, why have you forsaken me?"), which is very similar to the Arabic: "Ilahi, Ilahi, lema taraktani?" (Mark 15:34). If you watched and listened to the Aramaic words in the film *The Passion of the Christ*, you have already heard and identified with Jesus' use of Elah and Alaha for God throughout the movie. Up to today, people from Aramaic Christian Syrian villages established in the first century continue to use the Aramaic language, including Elah and

Alaha, in their churches and homes. Millions of Christians of Arab origin do not have any problem with praying to God by His Arabic name, Allah. They agree wholeheartedly with the Moslem testimony that "there is no god but Allah," but they immediately add **"in Christ."**

This testimony that "there is no god but Allah" is similar to the declaration in the Torah that "the Lord is God; there is no other besides him" (Deuteronomy 4:35), and to God's word through the prophet Isaiah that says, "Before me no god was formed, nor shall there be any after me" (Isaiah 43:10). These are just a few among many other similar declarations in the Old and New Testaments.

● ●

To Think about and Discuss

1. Before having read this chapter, if someone would have asked you, "Who is Allah?" what would have been your immediate answer?

2. What is the author's point about Allah as one of the names for the true God?

3. How are the words: Elohim, Allahu, Elah, Alaha, and Allah linguistically related?

Were There Pre-Islamic Arabian Christians?

*E*ven though history was not my favorite subject in school, I now find myself running to the history books trying to understand what I read in the newspaper or see on CNN. We can't forget that the spread of religions and materialistic philosophies, as well as conquering military powers, have influenced and at times completely changed the landcape of a country and the history of a people.

The descendents of Lot, Ishmael, and Esau (all from Abraham's family), along with other nomadic peoples took with them the knowledge (either combined with other orthodox teachings or at times combined with heresy) and name of the true God into the vast deserts of Negeb, Sinai, and Arabia. The Jews had carried their religion with them as they spread out geographically in the entire Middle East because of trade, persecution, and famine. Their presence formed a base of knowledge about the one true God upon which Christians built as they obeyed Christ's command to witness to the uttermost ends of the earth (Acts 1:8).

This spread of Christianity in what is today known as the Arab world started even from the first century with the preaching of Paul in Damascus and during the time he spent in Arabia probably among other Jews, and the evangelization of the Middle East and North Africa by the other apostles and followers like Saint Mark (writer of the gospel of Mark) who began the evangelization of Egypt. Simon, who helped to carry Jesus' cross (Matthew 27:32), and Lucius, one of the men at Antioch who ordained Paul for his missionary endeavor (Acts 13:1-2), were noted to be from Cyrene (present day Libya), and are probably ancestors to Libya's current president, Muammar Qadhafi.

There were Jews and Christians (either orthodox or members of various sects with false teachings) living and/or trading in Arabia in the six centuries between the death of Christ and the birth of the prophet of Islam. *Operation World* notes this about the present-day center of Islam: "Saudi Arabia once had a large Christian population. They were expelled when Islam gained control 1,300 years ago."[6] Stories from the Bible translated into Arabic had been narrated to the local inhabitants who worshipped a variety of gods. In the religious center at Mecca there were many idols representing these gods; among them was a statue-less place reserved for "Allah" who was known as the sovereign universal creator not made by hands. It has been noted that there were several inhabitants of Arabia who had left polytheism for the monotheistic worship of Allah and were clearly influenced by Christian and Jewish teachings. One of these Christians was Waraqah, a relative of Khadija, the first of the Moslem prophet's wives. Even the name of the father of the prophet was *Abd Allah* (the slave of God).

There is no doubt, however, that people living in pre-Islamic Arabia differed in their concepts of Allah. Even among Jews, nominal Christians, and false Christians (members of various cults), the understanding of God (Allah) must have ranged from a very distant non-personal power that somehow, somewhere controlled the universe, to the more relational God who involved Himself in the daily affairs of His followers in mighty acts of deliverance. Some Arabic-speaking Christians were probably true Christians having what we describe as "saving faith in Christ."

It would be no wonder that also some local inhabitants from a polytheistic background would perhaps consider Allah as just another god, but much more universal. They had probably also been impressed with the claims of the one great God as taught in such Jewish and Christian scriptures as: "The Lord is a great God and a great king above all gods" (Psalm 95:3), "What God is great like our God?" (Psalm 77:13), and "Behold, God is so great" (Job 36:26), all of which in Arabic mean *Allah Akbar*. In fact, the Hebrew word used in Job 34:17 and 36:5 to describe God's greatness, *Kabeer* is exactly the same word in the Arabic language for *great* while *Akbar* is the Arabic word for *greatest*.

The Quranic writings of the seventh century very clearly indicated that there were at that time Jews and Christians in Arabia, even though history seems to indicate that they were not able to long withstand the increasing militaristic atmosphere that developed. The Quranic understanding is that Christians and even Jews of Arabia believed in the fact of the crucifixion of Jesus the *Christ,* translated *alMasih* in Arabic, and *alMesiha* in the Aramaic language (Sura 4:157, 171; 3:45). The Quran disagrees with Christian doctrine, but recognizes Christians as people who believe that Christ is the Son of Allah (Sura 9:30), and who claim Allah to be in three persons

(Sura 5:73). Thus, the Quran clearly identifies Christians as worshipers of Allah who were present and well-known in Arabia before the prophet and teachings of Islam came.

We know that the name Allah was the name for God used by Arabic-speaking Jews and Christians and that its use continues even after Islam and until now. For twenty centuries there is no other Arabic name for God that arose or was used by Christian Arabs. Thus, it is a historical fact that as Saal indicates, "Allah is simply the Arabic word for God; it is used by Arabic-speaking Christians as well as by Muslims. Allah is not the Muslim God *per se*, though it is important to remember that the Muslim conception of God differs from that of the Bible at several major points." [7] Also, we concur with Geisler and Saleeb who write: "We make no distinction ... as some do, between the word *Allah* and the English word *God*." [8] No evangelical Christian would doubt the spiritual and academic integrity of the great missionary Samuel Zwemer, who wrote: "In pre-Islamic literature, Christian or pagan, ilah is used for any god and Al-ilah (contracted to Allah), i.e., ... the god, was the name of the Supreme." [9]

To Think about and Discuss

1. What do we know from the New Testament about the spread of Christianity in the present day Islamic countries of Turkey, Lebanon, Syria, Jordan, Egypt, Libya, Saudi Arabia, and Palestine (Gaza and the West Bank)?

2. What were the Jewish and Christian influences on the emergence of Islam in the Seventh Century A.D.?

God – Name or Concept?

What Is the Issue?

When my family and I arrived in sub-Saharan Africa in the early 70s, we were surprised to find so many Christian believers among the people who had originally followed African traditional religions. We had the wonderful opportunity of living near Mzee Musa Shipiri one of the last living elders remaining from those first generation converts. It was fascinating to learn about the culture and history which he related concerning his tribe, the Abaluyia of western Kenya. For many years before Christianity entered East Africa, his tribe had worshipped, in addition to lesser gods and spirits, the obscure non-personal power in the sky without which there was no sun to give warmth and light and no clouds to give rain. As farmers and hunters, they were very dependent on that life-giving power without which, there was no life. This power was called *Nyasaye* in the Luyia language and was referred to as "the One to whom sacrifices are made (or paid)." [10] Every morning the older men of the tribe would arise early to pray: kneel facing east, spit as a sign of respect, and ask Nyasaye for his blessings. [11] They would kill a goat or other animal on behalf of their people as a sacrifice to appease that power to continue his *benevolence*. When missionaries later came and saw that, they told the people, "You are right to worship Nyasaye; but he is not just a great power or one among many gods. *He is the* **One and Only** true and personal God who gave the blood of His *Son whom He sent* down to earth to be your sacrifice in the place of your goats and oxen." As they went on to explain the teachings of the Bible, many of these Africans accepted this good news. For decades now these converted brothers are still using *Nyasaye* as the name for their triune God as revealed to them in the Bible. He is now, *Nyasaye in Christ*.

The same thing happened with the many other tribes in Kenya, Tanzania, and Malawi who worshipped the power in the sky they called *Mungu*. Today you will find that *Mungu in Christ* is the true God for millions of Swahili-speaking African Christians. What is wrong in using the name but now with the biblical concept replacing the old concept? Would you have wanted to tell them that they should think up a new name for God or use one from a foreign language? No, the name doesn't matter. It is the concept that is extremely important!

God has His own ways to show Himself through general revelation in nature and the traditions and history of ancient peoples. We are thankful that, as Don Richardson pinpoints and exemplifies, God has set a desire for eternity in all men's hearts (Ecclesiastes 3:11), thus preparing a way for them to later receive the special revelation found in the sacred scriptures (the Bible) and in the Word of God (Jesus Christ). Richardson estimates that at least ninety percent of the folk religions on this planet contain a clear belief in the existence of one supreme God even though each would probably have a slightly or vastly different name. [12]

We should not devalue the name of Allah by rejecting it as a legitimate name for God. If we visit an Arabic speaking Christian church here in the States or travel abroad to worship with the millions of Christians of Syria, Lebanon, Egypt, Palestine, and Jordan, we will be hearing nothing but sincere praise to Allah in Christ. They are offended to hear that many Western writers are saying that the name "Allah" refers only to the Moslem god. These Arabic-speaking Christians will never accept any other name except Allah for the one true God. *Yes, Allah in the Messiah, Jesus of Nazareth!* Thousands of Middle Eastern martyrs throughout history from the first century until now have given their lives for believing in Allah in Christ.

Let us put our efforts into clearly defining, explaining, and sharing the true concept of God with those who know Him by the same or any other name, but have an inadequate, incomplete concept. Let us pray that the Holy Spirit will soften hearts and bring a response. What are our nations, our churches, as well as we ourselves personally doing to correct incomplete concepts that have remained uncorrected for centuries?

Nominal Christians, those who consider themselves to be Christians but who are living lives of materialism, selfishness, and immorality, are *themselves* believing, living, and promoting a wrong concept of God for themselves and to others who will judge Christianity and the Christians' God by this type of attitude and behavior. Those who are the pastors and priests of these nominal Christians have an awesome calling to help make certain that they know the distinction between a false and the true God, and are providing good examples of being His children in their daily lives.

When we approach others with the biblical concept of God, we do not try to eliminate the name they are using for God or pressure them to find a new name. On the contrary, we help to fill in the missing information with explanations from God's revelation of Himself in the Scriptures, correct any misconceptions, and demonstrate a good testimony and example of what it means to live in relationship with the true God.

● ●

To Think about and Discuss

1. What other names for God are you aware of?

    Do they have the same concept as that of the God you know?

2. Which is more important, the name or the concept of God and why?

3. How do nominal Christians who supposedly know the biblical concept of God distort the true concept? (If you are a Jew or Moslem, is the true concept of Elohim or Allah being distorted by adherents of your religion?)

Map of Middle East Countries Where Christians Use "Allah" to Refer to the Triune God

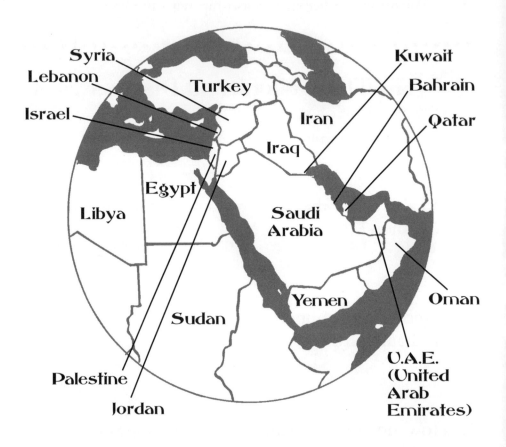

Middle East Countries Where Christians Use "Allah" to Refer to the Triune God

Country	Number of Christians	Percent of Population
Bahrain	63,944*	10.36
Egypt	5,887,366	12.98
Iran	220,000	0.33
Iraq	358,281	1.55
Israel	115,238	2.25
Jordan	183,407	2.75
Kuwait	161,082*	8.17
Lebanon	1,047,875	31.93
Libya	168,142*	3.00
Oman	64,560*	2.54
Palestine	65,793	1.94
Qatar	62,722*	10.47
Saudi Arabia	980,044*	4.54
Sudan	6,838,666	23.19
Syria	825,580	5.12
Turkey	213,091	0.32
U.A.E.	225,833*	9.25
Yemen	9,056*	0.05

Total Christians in these Countries 20,491,580

* mostly from other Arab and Asian countries

Statistics taken from *Operation World, 21st Century Edition*

PART II

God's Greatness: How Far beyond the Limits?

Is Allah Akbar in the Old Testament?

*I*n discussing the concept of God with Jews, Christians, and Moslems, I have never met a single one who would disagree that one of the major characteristics of His nature is His sovereignty and power. Whether in Mexico City, Boston, or Beirut, you cannot conclude even a discussion on the topic of business without someone expressing—*God willing*, *primeramente Dios*, or *insha'Allah*—to remind you that man can plan, but only God can make it happen.

Elohim Kabeer in the Hebrew language means that God is so great and powerful; [13] which is the same meaning as Allah Akbar in the Arabic language. For Jews in the Old Testament period, God, whether known in Hebrew as El or Elohim (God), Yahweh (Jehovah), or Adonai (Lord), was always the greatest and only God. He was known as Allah in Arabic, and Alaha in Jesus' native tongue of Aramaic. For all, His sovereignty was beyond imagination and comprehension.

Thousands of years before Islam came into existence, the equivalent to the Moslem testimony that "there is no god but Allah" (La ilah illa Allah), is found in several places in the Jewish religious books: (2 Samuel 7:22; 2 Samuel 22:32; 1 Chronicles 17: 20; Psalm 86:10). The description of Allah as being the most merciful (ar-*Rahman,* ar-*Rahim*) is repeated numerous times (Deuteronomy 4:31; Nehemiah 9:17b, 19a; Daniel 9:9; Psalm 86:15) where He is portrayed as ready to forgive, gracious, slow to anger, and having great mercy.

For the Jews, God *Is*; His existence is the undisputed fact. For centuries the Torah, when translated into the Arabic language, has started with the words, "In the beginning Allah created the heavens and the earth" (Genesis 1:1). Allah is described as the *I Am* (Exodus 3:14) who has been and will always be, and as Elohim Kabeer, the Great God in His creation and ownership of life (Psalm 24:1).

He is Akbar or *Almighty* in His sustenance of life (Acts 17:28), and in His awesomeness as everlasting (Genesis 21:33) and eternal (Psalm 90:2). He is the Greatest in His self revelation: "The heavens are declaring the glory of God; and the firmament proclaims his handiwork" (Psalm 19:1). Much, much more could be said about His omnipotence, omnipresence, and other attributes.

In God's providential solution for humanity, He called and chose Abraham and his descendents to be instruments through which the world would be blessed. He provided the ram to be sacrificed in place of Abraham's son, Isaac (Genesis 22:2), which was pointing towards the final, best, and only sufficient sacrifice: the Lamb of God, the coming Messiah, Jesus of Nazareth, through whom all who believe would be saved (John 1:29).

In the sacred Jewish scriptures, the term Messiah or "anointed one" referred to a person anointed with oil, symbolizing the power of the Holy Spirit which would enable him to do what God called upon him to do. As time passed, God began to reveal through the prophets that He would be sending from Himself to earth one specific unique Messiah to be born through the lineage of King David, who through the power of God's Spirit would accomplish a very special task for all humanity.

Some Jews believed this task was to have a military or political objective, while others believed it to be spiritual. Many hopes and dreams were built upon the prophecies concerning this expected person. The present-day Jews who reject Christ (from the Greek word *Christos* which means "Messiah") need to prayerfully read the Old Testament prophecies and ask Jehovah to open their eyes and understanding.

The only one who was to come, the only person who was so often prophesied about in the Torah and other Old Testament writings, was the Messiah. However, the majority of influential Jewish religious leaders did not recognize Him even though their prophets had promised among other things:

.... a child to be born who is "Mighty God" (Kabeer),
.... a child who is also the "Everlasting Father."
(Who could be Greater, more ***Akbar*** than that?)
.... a child whose name would be called,
.... "Wonderful Counselor," and "the Prince of Peace."
(Isaiah 9:6)

Old Testament Prophecies Concerning the Messiah That Were Fulfilled by Jesus Christ in the New Testament

• •

Old Testament Prophecy	New Testament Fulfillment in Christ
To be the promised seed of Isaac	
Genesis 17:19	Matthew 1:2; Luke 3:34
Heir to the throne of David	
Isaiah 9:7; 11:1-5; 2 Samuel 7:13	Matthew 1:1; 12:23; 21:9
To be born in Bethlehem	
Micah 5:2	Matthew 2:1; Luke 2:4-7
From a virgin	
Isaiah 7:14	Matthew 1:18; Luke 1:26-35
Specific time of birth	
Daniel 9:25	Luke 2:1-7
To be the Son of God	
Psalms 2:7; Proverbs 30:4	Luke 1:32; Matthew 3:17

Old Testament Prophecy	New Testament Fulfillment in Christ
Will perform miracles	
Isaiah 35:5-6	Matthew 11:3-6; John 11:47
To be rejected by Jews	
Isaiah 53:3; Psalms 2:2	John 1:11; Luke 4:29
Triumphal entry to Jerusalem	
Zechariah 9:9; Isaiah 62:11	Matthew 21:1-11; John 12:12-14
To be betrayed by a friend	
Psalms 41:9	Mark 14:10; Matthew 26:14-16
Hated without a cause	
Psalms 69:4; 109:3-5	John 15:23-25
Suffered for others	
Isaiah 53:4-6,12	Matthew 8:16,17; Romans 4:25; 1 Corinthians15:3
Crucified with sinners	
Isaiah 53:12	Matthew 27:38; Mark 15:27-28; Luke 23:33

Old Testament Prophecy	New Testament Fulfillment in Christ
Hands and feet pierced	
Psalms 22:16; Zechariah 12:10	John 20:25; 19:37
His side was pierced	
Zechariah 12:10	John 19:34; 20:27
His resurrection	
Psalms 16:10;	Matthew 16:21; Matthew 28:9; Luke 24:36-48
His ascension	
Psalms 68:18	Luke 24:50-51; Acts 1:9
To be at the right hand of God in Heaven	
Psalms 110:1	Matthew 26:64; Hebrews 1:3

These are only some of the over three hundred Messianic prophecies fulfilled by Jesus of Nazareth. It has been estimated by using the scientific law of compound probabilities that the odds of one person fulfilling just eight of these is one in ten to the seventeenth power (1 in 10^{17}). The slightest chance of this ever happening has been described in the following example:

"(Suppose) we take ten to the seventeenth power silver dollars and lay them on the face of Texas (an area double the size of Iraq). They will cover all of the state two feet deep. Now mark one of these silver dollars and stir the whole mass thoroughly, all over the state. Blindfold a man and tell him that he can travel as far as he wishes, but he must pick up (only) one silver dollar and say this is the right one. What chance would he have of getting the right one? Just the same chance that the prophets would have had of writing these eight prophecies and having them come true in any one man, from their day to the present time." [14]

This most unique Jesus of Nazareth was the only person who fulfilled in His life history all these specific areas which had been prophesied! No other prophet from any other religion comes even close!

To Think about and Discuss

1. Where in the Old Testament, which was written thousands of years earlier than the Quran, are found two of the most important testimonies for Moslems:

   A. "There is no god but God (El, Elohim, Adonai, Yahweh)."

   B. "God (Elohim, Eloah, El Shadai) is the greatest."

2. What other Messianic prophecies from the Jewish Scriptures were fulfilled by Jesus of Nazareth, along with those already quoted by the author?

3. Jesus of Nazareth was very much aware of these Old Testament prophecies. Which prophecies did Jesus Himself refer to before His death? After His resurrection?

Is Elohim, Allah in the New Testament?

*M*y wife who is a teacher told me that she never knew how much she didn't know until she entered the first classroom that had students who not only asked, "What?" or "When?"; but had questions of "How?" and "Why?". How many questions of this type do we have about God? Thankfully, He is able and willing to help us find the answers.

The long-awaited one, the Messiah, finally came in the time of God's own choosing through the only virgin birth recorded in history. Why not? Isn't God the sovereign Lord who can do anything He wills, as even the Quran repeatedly says? Even from a virgin without a husband. When Mary asked how this could be possible since she had no husband, the angel Gabriel told her, "The Holy Spirit will come upon you, and the power of the most High will overshadow you; therefore the child to be born will be called holy, the Son of God" (Luke 1:35).

This does not mean (as some have erroneously believed or questioned) that God had sexual relations with Mary. God forbid! There was nothing sexual in the conception of Jesus (Isa)! Even the Quran describes Jesus' birth as unparalleled, saying that into the virgin woman (Mary), "we (Allah) breathed of our spirit, and made her and her son a sign to all the nations" (Sura 21:91). (Note the Quran's use of the plural forms of *we* and *our* in the speech of Allah here and elsewhere.) Yes, this son is Jesus Christ, the only person in all human history born supernaturally and directly from God, through a virgin woman; not by sexual means, but by God the Holy Spirit. God is Spirit, but entered human history visibly apparent in Jesus Christ as the name given Him implies: *Immanuel*, which means *God with us* (Isaiah 7:14; Matthew 1:22-23). However, Judaism which proudly proclaimed to the world that Elohim is Kabeer, along with Islam and other religions and sects (e.g. Jehovah's Witness), disagrees emphatically with this main biblical and apostolic Christian doctrine of Incarnation.

The question is: "Is there any other person in all history like Jesus Christ?" No, there is no comparison between Him and any other human being The Spirit of God who had been present in the world since creation, entered our human situation and identified with our predicament through the person of Jesus Christ. If God is *so* Great, Allah Akbar, Elohim Kabeer, can anybody say *No* to God, the Greatest? Can we say *Impossible*! to *Him*? How can we (mere men) limit *Allah* al-Qadir who is by all definition — the Able, the Greatest, *Kabeer/Akbar*, and unlimited — by saying that He cannot be whatever He wants to be? Isn't it a huge sin for us to say that Elohim, Allah, God, cannot be such and such? Just for the sake of comparison, how can the mind of the small ant even comprehend the greatness of an elephant, or a whale? Would its brain be able to limit the very essence of either an elephant or a whale? Are we capable, or even permitted to know everything about God the Greatest? Has God revealed all there is to know about Himself?

With our limited minds, we cannot say, "God is just so and so, but cannot be this or that." The All-Knowing God is still keeping some mysteries to Himself. If God is truly God, He can be whatever He wants to be! If God is truly God, He has the authority to decide which portion of His secrets He will reveal, including mysteries concerning His own nature. He is not obligated to disclose everything about Himself and His purposes, including the details of logic and the methods by which He chooses to accomplish them. Elohim, Allah, whose personhood and mind is much greater (Akbar) than all our human knowledge combined, knows that our minds cannot digest it all. The Sovereign God of the universe is not accountable to us, His creation, but we are accountable to Him, to accept by faith with thanksgiving what He has already shown us about Himself. "The secret things belong to the Lord our God, but the things revealed belong to us and to our children forever" (Deuteronomy 29:29).

> **If God is God, He can be whatever He wants to be!**

Do we not realize our own earthly human limitations? Have we already comprehended all that God has revealed to us in His creation? Have we already understood *all* that is surrounding us in earth, under the oceans, and in space, that we can arrogantly claim to have completely understood also the mysteries of God's own personhood?

Have we already understood fully the workings of our own human bodies?! Can we even put into words the principles behind how our eyes are able to communicate to our brain which records the picture of the rose we saw this morning, and can bring its memory back while we lie in our beds in the dark of the night? Do we already understand *all* the workings of our own minds, emotions, and souls so that we can jump so quickly to a conclusion about God's mind and will? Are we such geniuses that we are wise and thoughtful enough to conclude that Allah, Elohim, cannot be so Great (Akbar, Kabeer) and so loving at the same time that He could not send His unique being in a human body?

It is very easy to understand that a beggar cannot become a Crown Prince. He would not have the facilities (without the aid of Hollywood) to educate himself, give himself the correct knowledge of court affairs, manners, and dress. However, it is possible for a Crown Prince to put on old, dirty, torn clothes, leave his palace, go into the market place, try to identify with the poor, needy, sick, discouraged, destitute, oppressed, persecuted, hungry, naked, wounded, and depressed people of his kingdom. In fact it has been done by earthly kings and princes, we are told, for very short periods of time in human history.

When we think of the greatness of the power and wisdom of God, why is it so difficult to think of His greatness in the areas of love and self sacrifice? Maybe it is because we know how undeserving people are and how ugly and ungrateful we can be.

One of the most beautiful examples Jesus used in demonstrating the love of God and the limitless extent to which He will go in order to forgive and restore man, is what is called the story of the Loving Father and the Prodigal Son (Luke 15:11-32). As it is for us, it was similarly difficult for the Jews listening to the story to think that an honorable man after raising his son and giving him all his rights and privileges of inheritance could be so publicly dishonored, rejected, and disobeyed by that same son. However, the improbability and the wonder in the story lies in the father's attitude of sacrificing his rights (to guard his honor and protect his reputation before the family and community, to justly punish evil, and to refuse to forgive), because of his desire to restore the son to himself. Can you imagine an honorable elderly rich man in a Middle Eastern village, with his long robe caught up in his teeth in order to free his legs for a fast run down the road to meet and hug his wayward, dirty, and pig-contaminated son who was shamefully and slowly returning home? The father was risking the laughter of children and servants, women hiding their faces in embarrassment as they see his bare legs, neighbors ridiculing this unheard-of spectacle; all in order to make it very clear and public that he welcomed his lost son, accepted him, forgave, and restored him.

Yes, it was the Almighty *God* who left the glory of heaven to reach out to His lost children by putting His Spirit into the womb of Mary and bringing forth the Messiah, God in the flesh. Yes, Elohim is so Kabeer, Akbar in Christ! God as we know Him through Jesus Christ's teachings and personal example is great in His power, love and self-sacrifice.

Earlier in history God had given Jews the law of Moses, sent the prophets one after the other, redeemed the people from slavery in Egypt and from Babylon, and conquered their enemies from the Nile to the Euphrates and beyond, considering them as His chosen people who were to be His instrument to save the world. Yes, Elohim intended for Israel to be His hands and feet to serve and save the world; but Israel failed. They thought that at the same time they were disobeying and betraying Him in sin, they could appease Him with their sacrifices, prayers, fasting, and external religious piety. However, through the prophets He condemned these few but influential wicked Jewish leaders by telling them, "I desire obedience rather than sacrifice" (1 Samuel 15:22-23).

Satan (whom the Bible calls our adversary, the deceiver, and the father of lies) has a grip on human nature so strong that even after following every ritual for cleansing, man finds himself returning to the same or even worse sin. The evil world system, the temptations from Satan, and weak human nature are such that man could not overcome them in his attempt to please God, who is also the Greatest in Holiness. People could neither keep themselves from sinning nor save themselves from the punishment for their sins! Their strong inclination towards selfishness and the constant need for immediate fulfillment of their fleshly desires, went hand in hand to ensure their defeat. They found themselves unable, regardless of how much and how often they prayed, fasted, and gave offerings to God, to remove their deep instinct for unlawful fulfillment of their desires. No amount of good works could wipe away the stain of their evil.

God was not surprised with this hopeless condition of man; so He, Allah al-Hakim, (the Wise) whose wisdom is much Akbar than ours, gave the "down to earth" solution in the manner of His own choosing. Yes, the Crown Prince can become a homeless beggar and can reach out to us – the filthy, needy, and miserable – in order to do for us what we cannot do for ourselves. In the time of His own choosing, God said, "Enough is enough! I knew from before the time of Adam that man would not be able to save himself. I will do what needs to be done; what they cannot do for themselves."

The Crown Prince came down in a unique manner never before nor again repeated in history He lived in a body like us; He gave; He touched orphans, widows, the sick, the grieving, and even the dead. He taught with beautiful lessons and corrected the misconceptions people had about Allah and what it means to live in a daily loving relationship with Him and with our neighbors.

Elohim, Allah, can and did come in Christ! If God is God, He can be whatever He wants to be, even if this is not the traditional concept of Him that we have always had. Is it too difficult for us to think of *Him* as a God of relationship and action, not just a God who gives orders and directions to others from a distant heavenly ivory tower? Remember, God is so great! *He* is much greater than our ideas, thoughts, preconceived theories and philosophies, even though they may be very *religious*.

• •

To Think about and Discuss

1. What is distinctive or different in the New Testament's concept of the greatness of God?

2. Read the story of the loving father and the prodigal son (Luke 15:11-32). What was Jesus trying to teach in this parable?

3. Why was it difficult for Jews to recognize Jesus of Nazareth as their long-awaited Messiah?

4. What are the Islamic objections to the New Testament's witness that God became flesh?

The God of the Ninety-nine Names

hen my son was young, he asked about what the different people were saying whom he had seen fingering the beads in their hands. My answer was, "If in Latin America, it was probably the Catholic rosary being recited, but if it was in the Middle East it was probably the ninety-nine names for God; these are some of their acts of worship.

"Bism Allah, ar-Rahman, ar-Rahim." — "In the name of God, the Merciful, the Compassionate." What a wonderful description and names for God! He is also similarly called al-Halim (the Kindly), ar-Rauf (the Gently Compassionate), and al-Wadud (the Intimately Compassionate). No vocabulary can ever be rich enough to describe our Great God (Allah Akbar) who has in Islam been described by ninety-nine names. [15]

In the Old and New Testaments we find most of these ninety-nine attributes or descriptions of God in functional format even though some may not be put as concrete names. You will find that every good and beautiful adjective has been used to describe the character of God and the encounters of the Almighty with His creation in history.

Millions and millions of people since the first century A.D. have been experiencing this rich and all-encompassing God through the Son, Jesus Christ, and through Him have come to call Allah, in addition to the ninety-nine beautiful and powerful names, the additional names of Father, Love, and Savior.

• •

To Think about and Discuss

1. Search the Old and New Testaments for attributes and characteristics of God and list them here.

1. What were the meanings behind the names for God in the Old Testament, such as: El Shaday, El Olam, Adonai, Yahweh, and others?

1. In your personal prayer life, what names for God do you use most often? Why?

Is Elohim, Allah, Our Father?

My first memory ever from early childhood was of being in my father's arms as he carried me to safety during the German bombing of World War II. In the midst of deafening explosions, I felt very small but secure in the strength and warmth of my *Big Dad*.

In the writings from the Psalms God is compared to an earthly father in His pity for His children: "As a father pities his children, so the Lord pities those who fear him" (Psalm 103:13). In the writings of the prophets He is recognized as the Father of all men by means of creation. "O Lord, thou art our Father; we are the clay, and thou our potter; and we all are the work of thy hand" (Isaiah 64:8). In the New Testament we see the use of the more intimate term for Father which is "Abba" in both Aramaic (the language spoken by Jesus) and Arabic (Romans 8:15; Galatians 4:6). This is an extraordinarily common name found in the mouths of babbling infants as they form their first words symbolizing love and trust. It was used by Jesus as he prayed alone with God in the Garden of Gethsemane (Mark 14:36), and this may have been the first time any religious leader is recorded to have used this intimate term to call upon the Great God of the universe!.

Through a relationship with Jesus, the Messiah, those who accept him are called children of God (John 1:12). This is a spiritual relationship resulting from the action and power of God's Spirit, not a physical relationship resulting from the action or will of the flesh. We become God's children by our spiritual rebirth (John 3:3) into His family. This covenant is sealed with the blood of Jesus Christ, by whom we are invited and enabled to call Allah Akbar by the new name of Abba, Father. As spiritual children of God we are not His slaves; we call Him Father instead of Sir or Master. This is a big contrast to slaves who in the Jewish culture were forbidden to address the head of the family by the title of Abba (Father). [16]

Many Moslems believe it is an honor to be called a slave of God, therefore, many of their names start with the word *Abd* which in Arabic means slave. Abd Allah means slave of God, Abd al-Khalik means the slave of the creator, Abd ar-Rahman means the slave of the merciful, and Abd al-Ghafur means the slave of the forgiver. No matter how beautiful those names might sound, in reality a slave does not have rights like a son or daughter; and he has no rights of inheritance. Through Allah's Christ we are guaranteed the best inheritance that allows us to enter the Kingdom of God for eternity: "So through God you are no longer a slave but a son, and if a son then an heir" (Galatians 4:7). This inheritance is not a physical one which would be subject to theft, the destruction by time of rust, mold, or moth, a decrease by age in beauty and strength, a de-evaluation, and ultimately our death. The blessings of the inheritance that a child receives from God the Father begin immediately and are not all postponed for the future in heaven. Even in this life the child experiences the relationship of love and companionship with the Father through His Holy Spirit who lives with and in the child (Romans 8:14-17). No place in the Bible or in any other religious book, is this made more clear than in Romans 8:15: "For you did not receive a spirit that makes you a slave again to fear, but you received the Spirit of sonship. And by him we cry, *Abba, Father.*" The child experiences the peace and confidence of being in the family of God headed by his Father. He no longer relates out of fear, as a slave to a slave master, but as a son he dares to ask his Father in confidence for whatever he needs. Christ taught that God's children must learn to trust the Heavenly Father, as children trust an earthly father. No one but Jesus could make it any clearer: when children ask for bread, they do not expect to be given a stone, or when asking for an egg to be given a scorpion (Luke 11:11-12). The father-son relationship is diametrically different from that of master and slave. The differences may not be obvious from a superficial observation of the son and the slave working side by side on the task they have been assigned. But there is a huge difference in their attitudes, motives for obedience, knowledge of the father's plans, and expectations of future rewards. Jesus said that His followers were not His slaves, but His friends. To prove this, He revealed Himself to them in a personal way that a master would never confide to a slave. He told them that His love for them made Him willing to lay down His life on their behalf (John 15:12-15).

Later the apostle Paul explained that both the Jews who were under the burden of the Law and the Gentiles who were under the control of pagan spirits were similarly in bondage to sin and Satan and were in need of freedom. For this reason God had sent a Redeemer, the Christ, to purchase these slaves so that they might become God's children.

God, Allah Akbar, forgives, not as a master to a slave, but as a Father who knows His daughter's or son's inclination for disobedience and wrong. He knew that the only way to make His children free from their bondage to sin was by paying the ultimate price of shed blood (that of Jesus Christ) to release them.

A tragedy arises when some slaves do not share their master's confidence that the relationship could be changed to that of a father and child. They are not convinced of his genuine love and desire that would enable them to enter his family. We have heard of slaves who out of a slave-complex and fear of the unknown, refuse to be freed or after freedom have returned to slavery because they feel bound to be *bound* to the master. Their backs are geared to bend and bow. Their heads and eyes are accustomed to only look down and to kiss his feet. They find it difficult to look straight into the face of the master. On the contrary, sons look face to face to a loving father with great respect. His joy is in seeing their smiling faces and beautiful joyous eyes. His satisfaction is that of the loving father who ran to meet his prodigal son, lifted his son's guilty face, kissed him, and wrapped his arms around him. The father proudly, in the presence of all the village, walked home shoulder to shoulder with his son, the heads of *both* held high. The son, as a child was guaranteed all privileges of security, peace, and rights as a member of the father's family. Likewise the child of God is encouraged to come with confidence into the presence of his Father, God. When the true Christian prays and worships, he addresses God as his Heavenly Father (as Jesus taught in Matthew 6:9); we do not relate to Him or worship Him in a slave-master mode.

Followers of Christ, let us take note to walk in faith and

courage as sons and daughters and not fall back into slavery to external rituals and laws, or internal bondage to sin. "For freedom Christ has set us free; stand fast therefore, and do not submit again to a yoke of slavery" (Galatians 5:1). "For you were called to freedom, brethren; only do not use your freedom as an opportunity for the flesh..." (Galatians 5:13). Our Savior gives us positive encouragement to be faithful and stand firm in our new relationship, by reminding us: "If you hold to my teaching, you are really my disciples. Then you will know the truth, and the truth will set you free.... So if the Son sets you free, you will be free indeed" (Romans 8:31, 36). Take courage: a follower of Christ is no longer a slave to Satan and to his own weak flesh, but is a recreated or reborn child of God. How is this possible? Because, in addition to being the Father, He is Love.

● ●

To Think about and Discuss

1. How would you describe a slave's attitude toward his master?

2. What are the distinctive aspects of a father's relationship with his children?

3. Summarize the author's description of the relationship of a believer and follower of Jesus with God, the Father.

4. How does this differ from the relationship that adherents of other religious faiths have with God?

Is Elohim, Allah, Love?

*F*riends from differing language backgrounds try to convince me that their mother-tongue is something more special than others. Some have told me that English is the language of *business*, Arabic is the language of *God*, and Spanish is the language of *love*. If I could borrow from their words, I would express something like this: the *business* language of *God* towards man is *love*.

In the Old Testament we see the workings of a loving God on behalf of His people. "It was not because you were more in number than any other people that the Lord set his love upon you and chose you...but it is because the Lord loves you, and is keeping the oath which he swore to your fathers ..." (Deuteronomy 7:7, 8). He also said, "I have loved you with an everlasting love..." (Jeremiah 31:3).

In Christ of the New Testament it became clear that God does not just give love but that love is His very essence: "God (Elohim, Allah) is love" (1 John 4:8). This love includes but also goes beyond being *rahman* (merciful), *rahim* (compassionate), and *raouf* (kind). God is love in Christ who taught His disciples that true love is to sacrifice self, to serve others, and to give your life for your friends, and even your enemies.

It was love for his subjects that caused the Crown Prince to leave his palace and sacrifice his birthrights and privileges, to be unrecognized, pushed around, probably kicked, beaten by thugs who might have lost their minds and had been rubbed the wrong way by the new, strange beggar. He must have had to dip into the garbage to find any dirty leftover crumb to eat. He might have been harassed by the police or authorities, jailed, spat at, and caned. He might have slept on a cold hard floor and had to use a corner somewhere as a bathroom. At any time the Prince could have said, "This has gone far enough! I am going to tell them who I really *am*, get out of this misery, and punish those who are kicking me around." By the time he is even beginning to be tempted to contemplate the possibility of escape, he recognizes that he has emptied himself of his identity and the authority of his throne for this very purpose – self sacrifice on their behalf.

Our analogy can go no further, for as far as human circumstances are concerned, Allah's Messiah (different from the Crown Prince) had not just played the role of a simple commoner, but He had become one in order to fulfill the objective of Allah, the Greatest. In the back of His mind Christ knew that at any time He so desired He could call for legions of angels to come and reveal His true identity and power and claim *His* victory (Matthew 26:53-54). Yet, He resisted this use of His full divinity in order to allow His full humanity to endure the bitterness of the cup of suffering, even to the extent of the cross, and therefore complete the plan of salvation. Christ knew the full extent of the consequences of what this humiliation would mean for Him. He knew that the writers of the Psalms and the prophets had predicted that the Messiah would be counted among the sinners (Isaiah 53:12), that the religious rulers would take counsel together against Him (Psalm 2:2), and that He would be rejected and despised by men (Isaiah 53:3). The Messiah knew how some (not all) influential Jewish leaders would attack like wild dogs, and even how they would crucify Him by nailing His hands and feet (Psalm 22:16-18).

Why did He accept such self-destructive humiliation? Because of His *love* for His people, the masses throughout the world. He wanted to identify with them, feel as they do, suffer with them, and experience their human destiny. If He really loved them, He needed to complete the only possible solution for their painful, hopeless existence. Jesus Christ understood people not only because He was their Creator (Colossians 1:16), but also because He humbled himself and became man like them (Philippians 2:7). He knew them well enough to know they certainly were not guiltless in their response to the evils and temptations of their miserable circumstances. They were helpless without His intervention. He was the only one who had the resources available to set them free. Only *He* could ransom them by the power of substitution: the righteous for the unrighteous, His life and blood given in the place of theirs.

The religious Jewish leaders did not see, or did not want to see, even though it was written in their Scriptures, that by His wounds they and all the people of the world were to be healed (Isaiah 53:5). Later the Apostle Paul voiced it clearly: "For our sake he (God) made him (Christ) to be sin who knew no sin, so that in him (Christ) we might become the righteousness of God" (2 Corinthians 5:21).

How could one man's death be of sufficient value to replace and eliminate the spiritual death that billions of other men deserved? Oh, you've forgotten, this was no ordinary man; He was the Crown Prince, Himself. Because of who He was, His pure royal blood was the only acceptable sacrifice. Why? Jesus Christ had no sin for which to be punished and therefore, was not obliged, as other men, to die. He was the blameless, perfect offering who was able and willing to pay the penalty for the sins of His people. The Torah had made it clear that there would be no forgiveness of sin without the shedding of blood (Leviticus 17:11), so Christ's death on the cross was fulfillment of the prophet Isaiah's declaration that the sovereign God would be willing to lay the iniquity of us all on the Messiah's bleeding sacrificial body (Isaiah 53:6).

This perfect self-sacrificial love in action cannot be found in any other religion or philosophy, because none else than Elohim Kabeer, Allah Akbar, was able to demonstrate this—in Christ. Yes, it is because God is Almighty, that He in Christ could have the ability to sacrifice and endure the humility and suffering, even suffering on a cross! As it is written, "All this is from God who through Christ reconciled us to himself… that is, God was in Christ reconciling the world to himself, not counting their trespasses against them…" (2 Corinthians 5:18-19). The Almighty is sovereign in His will and in His power to accomplish His will through His Anointed One, the Christ. This plan of God has been called "the mystery of his will according to his good pleasure, which he purposed in Christ…according to the plan of him who works out everything in conformity with the purpose of his will (Ephesians 1:9, 11).

Yet, some of you might be saying: "Oh, no! Doesn't the cross portray that God (whom we all know is All-Powerful, Kabeer) is weak, and that His plan for the Messiah was defeated by men? This is impossible! To die is weakness, to be killed is humiliation. Elohim of Judaism, Allah of Islam would not plan, agree, nor participate in such a thing as surrendering to the cross! This is blasphemy! The Messiah could not be insulted, spit upon, whipped, nailed, and crucified! What kind of Elohim or Allah would allow that?"

The Scripture's answers to these objections are: "Who has understood the mind of the Lord or instructed Him as His counselor?" (Isaiah 40:13), and *"Christ crucified: a stumbling-block to the Jews and foolishness to the Gentiles,.... Christ the power of God and the wisdom of God. For the foolishness of God is wiser than man's wisdom, and the weakness of God is stronger than man's strength."* (1 Corinthians 1:23-25). If some are still persistent in their objections, are they saying that their logic is better than that of God? Are they saying that they can limit His powerful love by their ability to comprehend all of His wisdom?! Are they saying that Allah can not do the humanly unthinkable? Yet, haven't we heard stories of the mother who sacrificed herself by drowning in order to allow her child to take the only space in the rescue boat, or of a loving human father handing his daughter to the safety of the fire fighters, while he, himself, is left to die in the fire? If we can accept human beings sacrificing themselves, why do we limit God's love for His human creatures? Can't we believe that He can plan to provide a sacrifice on the cross in the person of the human/divine Christ? It is written: "He (Christ) had to be made like his brothers (human) in every way, in order…that he might make atonement for the sins of the people" (Hebrews 2:17).

When in the unbearable, unexplainable and unjustifiable pain that you and I sometimes have to endure, what better comfort can there be than to know that if Christ undeservedly went through that much, at least He understands what we are going through and will give us the patience and ability to endure it? "Because he (Christ) himself suffered when he was tempted, he is able to help those who are being tempted" (Hebrews 2:18).

Millions and millions of people have accepted the greatness of God's love as shown in the cross, and have appreciated it. They cry out with words like this: "Oh! Oh! God Almighty, Elohim Kabeer, Allah Akbar, how high, how deep, how extensive is your love! If your love is so great that you had Christ's open arms nailed to the cross in order to embrace me, the least I shall do is to love you in return and give myself to you. I submit ("ussalem" in Arabic) my life to you in gratitude and acceptance of your gift. Not because you simply sent prophet after prophet, religious book after religious book, but You came *Yourself* in the person of Christ! Not because we offer the blood of animal sacrifices, but because You, in Christ, became the *only* acceptable pure sacrifice offered once and for *all* times on behalf of *all*."

• •

To Think about and Discuss

1. Allah is described in the Quran as the Most Merciful. How does mercy differ from love?

2. Describe what the author gives as an example of the ultimate love of God.

3. How do you respond to God's love for you? Why?

Is Elohim, Allah, the Savior?

*T*he third unique name that is to be added to the ninety-nine names for God, is Savior! The children of Israel discovered that their God was their deliverer and savior in the midst of the physical and material dilemma they faced in terms of slavery in Egypt and elsewhere, from battles in wars, from famines, and natural disasters. The prophet Isaiah recorded Elohim's words as saying, "I am the Lord, and besides me, there is no savior" (Isaiah 43:11). In the New Testament Mary was told to name her son *Jesus* (English) which in Hebrew is *Y'shua*, and in Arabic is *Yasua* or *Isa*. The angel reminded her that the meaning of this name was **Savior** and was chosen because her son would be the spiritual Savior who would deliver all from sin, from the power of Satan! (Luke 1:31; Matthew 1:21). Throughout His life, Jesus had to struggle against people's expectations that He, the Messiah, would become the military protector/deliverer who would relieve them from the oppression, discrimination, and economic hardships which they were facing.

Elohim, Allah is the spiritual Savior! Why is it hard to believe that God the *wise* (Allah al-Hakim), God Almighty (Allah al-Jabbar), God the Creator (Allah al-Khaliq), God the

Just (Allah al-Adl), God the Pardoner (Allah al-Ghaffar), God the Able (Allah al-Qadir), the Holy God (Allah al-Quddus), God the Light (Allah an-Nur), and the Wide-Reaching God (Allah al-Wasi), would say, "It is time that I reach out in a new and more powerful way by stretching my hand to pick up my children from the pit of their sin? Why should I deliver only the Israelites as I did from their physical captivity in Babylonia, and again now from a mere temporary military dictatorship like Rome? Let me deliver not only the Israelites but all of humanity from their most dangerous enemy of all, Satan, in a once-for-all defeat!" Is it impossible for Allah, ar-Rahman, ar-Rahim (the Merciful and Compassionate) to use His Akbarness (*greatness*), His Qudrah (great ability), and His Ghaffarness (pardoning ability) to save humanity from captivity by Satan in a special plan of spiritual salvation? Is it any more difficult for Allah, who is so Akbar, to deliver in the realm of the spirit, than in the physical? He cannot be restricted from any arena in which He wishes to save and deliver His people, or can He? Can God be limited?

God cannot be denied His desire to save spiritually or physically, nor can He be denied His own unique plan and method for bringing about this salvation. Even though Pharaoh of Egypt fought against God's desire to deliver His people from slavery, and fought against His method of using Moses to lead their escape on dry ground through the midst of a sea, he was unable to spoil the plan of God even though he tried with all his governmental power. Supported by Egypt's religious system with its priests and magicians, all his army and chariots were unable to discredit and destroy God's messenger Moses and the people of God. Yet their Jewish descendents deny that God could plan whatever means He chooses for salvation. The majority of Jews are still unwilling to accept the prophecies that fill the Old Testament about the Messiah who was to be born from a virgin in Bethlehem and have as a title, Immanuel, God with us. Yet, God's Word and will are always fulfilled. In the fullness of time, Elohim sent His Messiah, Jesus the Nazarene, to spiritually deliver humanity from the chains of Satan who had kept them enslaved in the sin which would ultimately lead them to hell. Surely the Almighty Elohim has the right and freedom to make it possible for flesh and blood, just like any of the billions of other human bodies He has created but without the contribution of a man's sperm added to the woman's ovum, to embody the Savior of the world? Is this too hard for us to believe? We tend to forget that we are talking about *God*, not about ourselves. As the heaven is higher than the earth, His ways and thoughts are higher than and much different from ours (Isaiah 55:9). Mary (Mariam), Jesus' mother, was a chosen vessel in

> **Jesus spoke the local language, but spoke no evil.**

which this body grew and was formed to have bones, flesh, a brain, emotions, and everything else that humanity is endowed with, so that this baby born in Bethlehem some two thousand years ago was just like any other child. And yet, there was nothing common or ordinary about this Savior. As God had designed, He was full of the Holy Spirit and had within Him the nature of the eternal holy God. This unique combination of God's nature being clothed with a human body (known as the Incarnation) was never before or after repeated in human history: there is only One Savior!

Although Jesus (Isa) spoke the local language, He spoke no

evil. In fact, He spoke the words of God. Although He had all royal power, He humbled Himself to live as an ordinary powerless person serving others rather than being served. Instead of using His position within God's plan to force His teachings and plans on men, He depended on the leadership and timing of God, even when it meant suffering an early death which would be misunderstood by some as weakness and defeat.

Why would Elohim have planned for this unique person, the God-Man, who was able to live a perfect life without sin (Hebrews 4:15), and was obedient to every godly desire and attribute, to be at the same time fully human and therefore, susceptible to suffering and death? God is Spirit and therefore has no body and blood to pour out as a sacrifice for His children. So He sent the Messiah, His anointed one, who willingly gave Himself (that is, this body, which God had already prepared to be pleasing and acceptable to Him) as a sacrifice. "He did not enter by means of the blood of goats and calves; but he entered the Most Holy Place once for all by his own blood, having obtained eternal redemption" (Hebrews 9:12).

Are you saying, "Impossible! God forbid!?" Yes, your skepticism is understandable. After all, that is what Peter also said when he first heard of such a plan from the Christ: "*God* forbid, Lord: This shall never happen to you" (Matthew 16:22). Peter was not considering the spiritual benefit that would be gained from Christ's sacrifice, he was looking at things from a material/human viewpoint. He could not understand what value could come from Jesus' death. In effect, Peter was saying, "This shall never happen to me." He did not want to lose all the benefits and security he was receiving from being the leader of Christ's followers. When Peter and others were hungry, Jesus blessed a few pieces of bread and fed thousands, when Peter needed money to pay taxes, Jesus directed him to a fish that had inside a coin of sufficient value to pay the government, when Peter's mother-in-law was sick, Jesus healed her, and when Peter was about to drown in the sea, Jesus rescued him. Yes, Peter wanted to keep Jesus as a savior limited to meeting a few men's physical needs in a small limited geographical area and historical context. Peter was forgetting, as we all forget, the remainder of Christ's words which revealed the purpose and conclusion to this death plan, that after Christ's death he would "on the third day be raised" (Matthew 16:21). That third day, Resurrection Day, was the ultimate demonstration in all of history of Allah's public victory over Satan's limited power of evil and death, and would be available and applicable to men of every tribe and nation in any time throughout the ages! Unlike leaders of other religions whose significance and teachings are related only to cultural practices of a certain geographical area and past century, the Savior, Jesus Christ is universal and timeless! Even the Quran testifies to the blessed uniqueness of Jesus (Isa) in His birth, death, and resurrection: "And peace on me on the day I was born, and on the day I die, and on the day I am raised to life" (Sura 19:33).

Every other religious teacher or prophet has been known to have a place where his bones are resting. Yet, Allah's Messiah victoriously arose alive from the tomb and was seen by over five hundred people in His glorified body which was marked by the piercing of the nails and the sword. In this resurrected body He walked and talked with people and even ate with them, *after* having been dead and buried. He ascended to heaven where He is now alive for ever. This fact is even testified to in the Quran (Sura 4:158). It is evident that in Christ's resurrection the Kingdom of God had overcome the kingdom of Satan. The Crown Prince of Peace, who for a short time had made Himself a beggar, has provided peace with God and is now seated on the throne with God, at the right hand of Power or the right hand of the Mighty One (Acts 2:29-36; Revelation 22:1,3), just as He claimed He would (Matthew 26:64). What other religious leader ever claimed that after death he would share the throne of God in Heaven? When He later revealed Himself to John, the resurrected Christ was heard to say from heaven, "I am the Living One (al-Hayy); I was dead, and behold I am alive for ever and ever! And I hold the keys of death and Hades" (Revelation 1:18), and "I overcame, and sat down with my Father on his throne" (Revelation 3:21).

Yes, Allah of the ninety-nine names has at least three additional, eternally significant names: Father, Love, and Savior!

• •

To Think about and Discuss

1. Explain the religious blood-sacrificial system required by God as described in the Old Testament? (Leviticus chapters 4 and 16)

2. Do you understand that God can give His own solution for our sins (considering that our own good works are always inferior at their best) in such an *ultimate sacrifice* (Jesus Christ's death on the cross) on our behalf?

3. Does the seriousness with which God views sin, and the extent to which He went in order to deal with it on our behalf, surprise you? What have been the results when other religions/concepts of God view sin less seriously?

4. Why is the resurrection of Christ considered most vital to the salvation and victory over sin in the life of the Christian? Study the meaning of 1 Corinthians 15:17: "If Christ has not been raised, your faith is futile; you are still in your sins," and Romans 8:11: "And if the Spirit of him who raised Jesus from the dead is living in you, he who raised Christ from the dead will also give life to your mortal bodies through his Spirit, who lives in you."

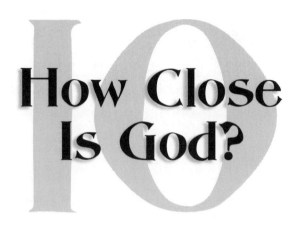

How Close Is God?

I once overheard an African friend ask his co-worker who happened to be a Mzungu (Swahili for *white person*), "Why are you angry with me?" "I'm not angry, I'm just exhaused from all this work we're doing," was the response. For this African friend *silence* from his co-worker meant that he did not care enough about their relaionship to *communicate*, even if both were tired. Yes, closeness between persons is measured by the communication, or lack thereof, from one to the other. How exhilarating to know that God *talks* to us in all situations and even more, perhaps, in our difficult times when we need it most. In the last days He spoke to us by His Son (Hebrews 1:1).

God, Elohim, Allah, the creator of man, has taken into account that man, made in His image, can best know God within relationships. If He is isolated and seen only from a distance, our Creator cannot be fully understood and appreciated by man in all His wonderful attributes. Some of them are known only within practical circumstances and situations that call forth their exhibition or use in action and reaction towards man.

Although God is Spirit, He has allowed Himself to be described with ordinary words as if He had a physical body with a face, eyes, and arms, so that men and women in their limited experience can understand and comprehend God in more concrete terms. He did not think it blasphemy to be described in human terms in order that His nature be understood. God Almighty had communicated the exact manner – including atonement and purification through animal sacrifices – by which man could gain His acceptance. When God relates to man, He is depicted as having emotions. He is described as being pleased and as blessing man, much as if He were smiling upon him: "The Lord make his face to shine upon you" (Numbers 6:25). On the contrary, when someone had disobeyed God, it was as if God had hid His face from him (Psalm 51:9). At one point, upon seeing the extreme wickedness and evil of man, it was said: "The Lord was grieved that he had made man on the earth, and his heart was filled with pain" (Genesis 6:6). God is described as if He has a human body. We are reminded that God's eye is always searching and examining His children to understand their inner motives (2 Chronicles 16:9). His arm was described as reaching out in power to save them from their enemies (Psalm 77:15), and His followers prayed that His ears would be open and attentive to their requests (Psalm 130:2).

God has not left man to guess, ponder, or theorize about who He is and what He is able to do. He has revealed Himself to people in multiple and various words and acts throughout history. In the Torah, the Writings (including the Psalms), and the Prophets, He revealed that He loves to relate to man and to call him near; but the obstacle was man's sin. Because God is holy (Quddus), there was a wall of separation and enmity between Him and impure man. That wall of separation was broken down when the blood sacrifice atoned for man's sin, and man was invited to draw near to God. The blood of lambs and goats, which were the yearly sin offerings prescribed in the Jewish scriptures, were later replaced by the once-for-all-time sacrifice of the Lamb of God (another name for the Messiah), Jesus of Nazareth. "But now in Christ Jesus you who once were far off have been brought near in the blood of Christ" (Ephesians 2:13).

As shown in the New Testament, part of Christ's mission was to correct the Jewish leaders' distorted traditional ideas about religious rituals and worship that kept the average man, woman, and child at a distance from God. Christ concentrated His teachings on how God loves and values all types of people. He described Satan as the enemy who deceives man by tempting him to rebel, resist, and draw away from God. Christ portrayed men as being sinners and therefore "lost" from the Father, and in need of a rescuer who would "save" them from the habitual power and penalty of sin. Jesus' purpose for coming was identified as being "to destroy the works of the devil" (1 John 3:8b), and to seek and to save that which had been lost (Luke 19:10).

Christ made a point of eating with sinners, calling the law breakers to follow Him; He even went as far as to clear the enmity between God and sinner, by forgiving sin! Any human being can forgive someone who has sinned against him personally. However, Christ was the only one who publicly pronounced forgiveness for sins that a person had made against others and against the holy God (Matthew 9:2-6; Mark 2:3-12; Luke 7:36-50). Even as He was dying on the cross, Jesus told the repentant thief hanging on the adjacent cross that the thief's sins were forgiven and that he would that same day be with Christ in paradise (Luke 23:43). This forgiveness would result in the thief being able to draw near to the very presence of God! Who can grant this type of forgiveness and entrance into heaven except God?

In the New Testament, Christ corrected the traditional Jewish religious teachings of that day that God did not want to relate to the sinner, the law breaker, or the sick. He explained that His miracles of healing were a proof that God, the Greatest, was the one working in Him to do these wondrous acts of kindness and power (John 9:4; John 10:24-25). In other words, the Christ was saying, "If you want to get the true understanding of how God relates to man, just listen to and watch me." Jesus also used word pictures that He knew would be considered as blasphemy: "He who has seen me has seen the Father" (John 14:9b), and "I and the Father are one" (John 10:30). This is the ultimate degree of oneness with God!

In the Quran, Allah Akbar, is also described in a manner that was easy for man to understand, but not always in a way that would draw men to him in a personal relationship. The prophet of Islam himself said that God lives in a house. The Quran talks about the face of Allah (Sura 2:115, Sura 55:26-27), and Allah's hand (Sura 48:10; Sura 57:29), and mentions Allah's eyes (Sura 11:37; Sura 52:48). But, the Quran also says that the Allah of Islam is cunning and deceitful (Sura 8:30), he orders people to do evil (Sura 17:16), he misleads some men so that they will be lost (Sura 14:4, 6:125), and that his desire is to fill hell with demons and men (Sura 32:13). If any reader can accept that the Almighty, called God or Allah, can have such human-like negative intentions for man, then how could he deny God the right and freedom to lovingly reveal Himself more completely and openly through the life of the perfectly pure Messiah? Consider to what great lengths God went in demonstrating His desire for man to be drawn close in loving relationship, and thereby escape the consequences of sin.

● ●

To Think about and Discuss

1. Where would Jews reading the Old Testament find some human attributes or features given for Elohim?

2. How can a Jew discover in Christ some of the closeness and forgiveness that he needs?

3. Where in the Quran are given some of the human characteristics of Allah? How does seeing and hearing the teachings of Isa (Jesus of Nazareth) help people to understand Allah and draw nearer to Him?

PART III

Jesus –
One of a Kind

The Greatness
of His Lifestyle

We are amazed when we examine the way in which the Christ lived His thirty-three years on this earth within the first century Middle-Eastern culture among followers of the Jewish religion. As Elohim in the flesh, He was not only described as the Son of God, but also as the Son of Man, (both names being titles for the Messiah). Although it was predicted in the Old Testament that the Messiah (haMoshiach in Hebrew and alMesiha in Aramaic, the language of Jesus) would be born of a virgin, this supernatural event was not accepted by the most influential Jewish leaders. They thought that He was born out of sin since His mother was not yet married to her intended spouse, and they hinted that the Christ was born out of an adulterous relationship (John 8:41). They demonstrated their ignorance when, confident of His merely human origin, they proudly declared that they knew He could not be the Messiah because they knew where He came from, and no one would know from where the Messiah would come (John 7:27). Yet, any Jew who studied the Old Testament knew that the Messiah was coming from a virgin (Isaiah 7:14) and was to be born in Bethlehem (Micah 5:2).

Jesus Christ's own lifestyle is incomparable; He had no pillow or bed on which to rest. He explained it like this: "The foxes have holes and the birds of the air have nests, but the Son of Man has no place to lay his head" (Luke 9:58). He clearly identified with the poorest of the poor, worked as a simple carpenter, and shared life with manual fishermen. He was the owner of all creation, but He chose to disown His royalty and live a common life so that we can appreciate the love and sacrifice that the Crown Prince made on our behalf. Occasionally the Christ would accept an invitation from a rich man to eat at his home, but only in order either to demonstrate God's love and desire to relate more closely to all, or to give an example of God's truth through His teaching. He did this when, in the home of a hypocritical religious leader, He forgave and commended the prostitute who showed her repentance by washing His feet with her tears and drying them with her hair (Luke 7:36-50). When Jesus went to the home of Zacchaeus, the rich tax collector, He called him to repentance, encouraged him to return what he had stolen and to give most of his wealth to the poor (Luke 19:1-10). His teaching was that repentance meant one must change his direction and dedicate all that he has for God and His people.

True religion is not to pray, fast, and give money or gifts to the synagogue, church, mosque, or other place of worship and then continue with some lying, insulting, backbiting, and cheating here and there; only to return again to more prayer and fasting. This is the never-ending human cycle of trying to appease God while at the same time willfully disobeying Him. Certainly Allah ar-Rahman, ar-Rahim, al-Gaffur, God the Greatest, is able to give men the power to repent for the past and to resist sin in the future. Surely it is not pleasing to a

Holy God when men try to use His mercy as a means of cheap grace in order to allow them to continue sinning. The Holy God hates sin, big or small! To the Christ, commitment to God brings joy in the single-minded purpose of pleasing Him, not sorrow in leaving evil ways, or money, or family, or power to follow Him. He taught that it is impossible to serve both God and anything else, including money (Matthew 6:24). Furthermore, once the choice for God is made, there is no turning back. "No one who puts his hand to the plow and looks back, is fit for the Kingdom of God" (Luke 9:62). What kind of crops can be produced if the farmer is looking backwards rather than looking ahead as he plows?

The life of Allah's Messiah was one of faith lived out in practical ways. He depended on God for His food and sustenance; He did not set out with His followers to attack others and take what was theirs. He taught that if God feeds the simple birds of the air, how much more He would care for us if we depend on Him. We do not need to live a life of anxiety and worry because God knows what we need even before we ask. If we really believe in God and put Him first in our priorities, He will meet our needs (Matthew 6:25-33).

Christ was the only person in history who, when some Jewish leaders accused Him of being under Satan's influence, could silence them by asking: "Who of you convicts me of one sin?" (John 8:46). His one hundred percent purity from sin meant that unlike any other human being, even a person with an excellent character, He had no need to be forgiven. Even His follower Peter, who was repeatedly rebuked by Elohim's Messiah, said about Jesus that "in his mouth was found no guile (deceit, cunning, treachery)" (2 Peter 1:22). Christ's enemies could not name any one specific sin with which to accuse Him except the false charge of blasphemy. Who, in all human history can match Him, morally? When a ruler came to Him calling Him "Good Teacher," He reminded them that there is none good but God (Luke 18:18), confirming that even they knew He was no ordinary man or even just a prophet. Other Jewish religious teachers (even while trying to trick Him) complimented Jesus (Isa) by saying, "Teacher, we know that you speak and teach rightly, and show no partiality, but truly teach the way of God" (Luke 20:21).

Even the Quran claimed for the Christ of Allah and for no other prophet, that He was miraculous (as a sign, "aiya") and sinless (pure or "zaki") (Sura 19:19-21). Sura 19:31 mentions that Christ was blessed wherever He was, meaning that God agreed upon His every action and word, every moment in His life. God would never bless anybody in every circumstance unless *all* his life was pure and sinless. In contrast, the Quran records its own prophet's confession that he was a sinner. The teachers of Islam quote their prophet's words that he used to repent one hundred times a day.

If Jesus was sinless, why was He accused, put on trial, and condemned to death? Humanly speaking, the Jewish religious authorities feared that His popularity with crowds of common people would cause the leaders to loose their egotistical control, as well as would encourage the people to revolt against Rome in an attempt to make Jesus their political ruler or king. The powerful Roman army might then destroy the nation of Israel and its Temple. The Jewish High Priest believed that by killing Jesus of Nazareth, this could be avoided. He, along with others, accused Jesus of blasphemy, a crime punishable in Jewish law by death. They charged that Jesus blasphemed when He claimed to be the Messiah promised from God (God in the flesh), thereby making Himself equal to God (John 5:18). The High Priest justified his actions by saying, "It is expedient that one man should die for the people, and that the whole nation should not perish" (John 11:50).

The Romans who were occupying Israel were not concerned about those breaking Jewish religious laws, only about those breaking Roman civil laws, however they were the only ones who had the right to execute law breakers by crucifixion. Therefore, these few Jewish leaders brought a false accusation that the Christ was a political threat to Rome. In order to get him condemned to death by crucifixion, they said that He claimed to be a king and was therefore a threat to the Roman Emperor. There was never an accusation that the Christ was a thief, an adulterer, a murderer, or had committed any other common sin. As fully human, He was tempted in everything like us, but without sin. As fully God, He resisted using His divinity to insulate Himself from being tempted by evil. As a complete human with needs and desires like yours and mine, Jesus was entirely vulnerable to temptation. Yet, He was in harmony with God's Spirit who continuously filled Him, cooperated with Him, and communicated with Him as He prayed in complete dependence on God, with the result that He successfully defeated all of Satan's temptations (Luke 4:1-13).

What were other differences about the way in which Christ faced Satan's temptations? When He was fasting forty days in the wilderness, Christ answered Satan's lies and mental suggestions by quoting to him the truth from God's Word, the Scriptures, which He had known perfectly from childhood even though He had not studied in a rabbinical school. Jesus met Satan's temptation that He avoid or escape suffering on the cross by praying for and submitting to God's will at this time of crisis. His practice of standing firm on the truth of God as revealed in Scripture, and by repeatedly seeking through prayer for God's will, is our true example today as the way for His followers to also resist Satan. Since He was tempted in everything like us, Christ must have had even visual temptations that tried to enter His eyes and senses, such as the sexual temptations that were surely around Him. He must immediately have turned His face the other way, one hundred eighty degrees, not giving His eye even an eighth of an inch chance to even glimpse at what could become the first step down the progression from the lust of the eye, to the thoughts of the flesh, to the act of sin. How do you compare that with you and me and all other men, even prophets or so-called prophets? Unlike others He never engaged Himself in any discussions, details, or teachings on sexual subjects. He, in contrast to other religious leaders, never taught that any man's or woman's bodily secretions could make them inaccessible to God. He focused on adultery as being the sexual sin that defiles a married man or woman in their relationship together as *one flesh* (Matthew 19:9).

Christ was greatly concerned with purity of the heart: "Blessed are the pure in heart for they shall see God" (Matthew 5:8). His concern was that men would worship God in spirit and truth (John 4:24). His teaching was that one might need to use extreme, unusual measures to avoid sinning, even to the removal of one's own right eye or own right hand if they are causing one to sin. This was Jesus' attempt to emphasize figuratively the horror and consequences of sin (Matthew 5:29-30). We have heard of religious laws in some countries calling for the cutting off of a thief's hand, but has anyone ever heard of someone cutting off his own hand because he had used it in some type of sin?

Christ was like His human ancestor Joseph, who literally ran from the Egyptian Pontifar's wife rather than sin against God by committing adultery. Yet Joseph was by no means close to the purity of Jesus Christ. Joseph's descendents, the Israelites, never claimed that Joseph was sinless either before or after this momentary victory in his life. We know that Joseph got married as other prophets and religious leaders do, and enjoyed physical relationships with his wife. Yet, Christ's pleasure was in communicating with the Father and doing His will as He served and sacrificed for those in need. When His disciples urged Him to stop ministering to people in order to eat something, He told them, "I have food to eat that you know nothing about.... My food is to do the will of him who sent me and to finish his work" (John 4:31-34).

By His teachings and perfect example Christ demonstrated the power of God over all types of evil. We who know our own weaknesses in the face of temptation, as well as those of our ancestors and children, can easily recognize that it is the holiness of none other than the Holy God (Allah al-Quddus) that we see in the consistency of the astonishingly sinless and pure life of Christ.

To Think about and Discuss

1. What were some of the human weaknesses and sins that we can see in the lives of great Jewish patriarchs and prophets (i.e. Abraham, Jacob, Moses, David, and Solomon)?

2. Can you recall any of the human weaknesses of the prophet of Islam?

3. How did the life of Jesus differ from that of these other religious leaders?

The Greatness of His Miracles

Restoring Human Bodies

When trying to recall the earliest seeds of faith in God's power that were planted in my boyhood, I cannot forget the healing miracle that happened in my family. My mother asked me, a nine years old, to kneel with her in a small room to pray for my hospitalized father, who was expected to die after a serious excision of a large part of ulcerated stomach. The internal stitches had come apart due to his severe hiccoughs, and the doctors said his grave condition would not allow them to re-operate for re-closure of the remaining stomach muscle. As my father lay half-conscious, Christ appeared to him, telling him to sit up, pick up his things and go home. The surprised doctors found him sitting; they X-rayed the stomach and found that it had closed properly. He began drinking, eating, and was soon at home praising God. Dad continued to live a full and useful life for twenty-three more years!

Throughout the Old Testament God did mighty miracles starting with the creation of the world before man even existed, and later in response to the needs and prayers of His people. He used the prophets of Israel to show His miraculous power, but no other religious leader or prophet in history has performed the miracles done by Jesus, Isa, Allah's Masih.

The difference from the prophet Elijah and the disciple Peter, who also raised the dead, is that the Christ did not have to ask in prayer for God to give Him the power to raise the dead. He already had that power. When Christ prayed before raising Lazarus, it was to give testimony to those watching that His power demonstrated in what He was about to do was a result of His relationship with God the Father (John 11:41-42). As fully human, Isa shed tears at Lazarus' tomb out of compassion for the two sisters' grief. But as fully divine He ordered, "**come out!**" to the body that had been four days in the grave. Much to the astonishment of the multitude, Lazarus came walking out still wrapped in the grave clothes! In another instance, because of compassion for the grief of the widow of Nain over the death of her only son, Jesus stopped the funeral procession that was carrying him to the grave, to raise him from the dead. (Luke 7:12-17).

Even the Quran witnesses that Jesus (Isa) was unique and incomparable with any other person. He was the only one in the Quran who was said to be able to do "bayenaat" (mysteries or miracles), (Sura 2:253). The Quran testifies that Jesus was able to give sight to the blind and heal the leper, in addition to raising the dead (Sura 3:49). Search the Quran and the Old and New Testaments for any other person who had such healing power that went out from him in response to a woman's desperate grasp of faith onto the back of his robe. She, who had thought, "If I just touch his clothes, I will be healed" (Mark 5:28), found that her bleeding of twelve years had stopped immediately — even before Jesus had a chance to turn around and see who had touched Him. Instead of rebuking her for making Him *religiously unclean* as the law prescribed, He lovingly called her "daughter" and told her to go in peace, freed from her suffering (Mark 5:34).

Who else ever had the authority to cast out the powerful demons/evil spirits from people? These spirits knew the identity and authority of Allah's Messiah and begged Him not to punish them before their time (Matthew 8:28-32). In the chart at the end of the chapter we can see in the list of the miracles of Moses, Elijah, Elisha, and those of Jesus, that Jesus was the only one of them recorded to have healed people of evil spirits and demons. Jesus also gave this power to His followers as well (Matthew 10:1).

As the creator and lover of men, the Christ had authority and power over all the diseases that attacked His creation. All manner of illness, even birth defects like blindness, were subject to His healing word or touch (John 9:1-7). He had no hesitation in touching persons having diseases like leprosy whom society had cast out as not only physically, but also spiritually unclean (Matthew 8:2-3). With a word, He healed ten lepers at once (Luke 17:12-14).

Jesus healed in absentia.

Another time, a Gentile army officer wishing to spare the Messiah from walking the distance and from becoming "impure" by entering a non-Jewish person's home, asked Him to "only say the word, and my servant will be healed." Christ's authority over the disease was directed by a word spoken even from a great distance and the sick person was instantly healed. Yes, He healed in absentia! No wonder Jesus praised the faith of this Gentile saying, "Not even in Israel have I found such faith" (Matthew 8:8-10).

The Spirit of God was seen by John the Baptist to descend upon the Christ at His baptism. At the start of His public ministry while in the Jewish place of worship, the Christ read from the prophet Isaiah beginning with these words: "The Spirit of the Lord is on me because he has anointed me to preach good news to the poor He has sent me to proclaim freedom to the prisoners and recovery of sight for the blind, to release the oppressed, to proclaim the year of the Lord's favor." When He finished reading, He concluded that, "Today this scripture has been fulfilled in your hearing" (Luke 4:18-21). He was concerned with all types of human problems, be they economic, social, physical, or spiritual. His miraculous actions on behalf of the people were initiated out of a deep personal compassion for their holistic needs as seen in Matthew 9:35-36: "Jesus went through all the towns and villages, teaching in their synagogues, preaching the good news of the kingdom, and healing every disease and sickness. When He saw the crowds, He had compassion on them, because they were harassed and helpless, like sheep without a shepherd."

Only Jesus Christ (Isa) is mentioned in the Quran as the one to whom Allah gave His Holy Spirit. The Moslem theologian Baidawi said that Jesus gave life to dead people and hearts; thus He was called "Spirit" (Sura 4:171).

While the sick, evil-possessed, and needy common people appreciated Jesus for His loving and miraculous acts of compassion, the influential Jewish religious leaders did not share their appreciation. Why was that? One reason is that several of these miracles were performed on the Sabbath day in contradiction to the interpretation of Jewish law which forbade man from working, even healing, on the Sabbath. Also, the miracles made Christ very popular causing great crowds of people to follow Him and to be open to His teachings which at times questioned the false interpretations and self-interest of the leaders. Another reason seems to be that the majority of the Jewish leaders had little, if any, concern for the poor and the weak who were being helped by Christ. Look at the following sharp confrontations that centered around Christ's miracles:

1. "So, because Jesus was doing these things (miracles of healing) on the Sabbath, the Jews persecuted him. Jesus said to them, 'My Father is always at his work to this very day, and I, too, am working.' For this reason the Jews tried all the harder to kill him; not only was he breaking the Sabbath, but he was even calling God his own Father, making himself equal with God" (John 5:16-18).

2. "Why then do you accuse me of blasphemy because I said, 'I am God's Son'? Do not believe me unless I do what my Father does. But if I do it, even though you do not believe me, believe the miracles, that you many know and understand that the Father is in me, and I in the Father. Again they tried to seize and stone him, but he escaped their grasp" (John 10:31-39).

3. "He who hates me hates my Father as well. If I had not done among them what no one else did, they would not be guilty of sin. But now they have seen these miracles, and yet they have hated both me and my Father. But this is to fulfill what is written in their Law: 'They hated me without reason'" (John 15:23-25).

Yes, it is obvious that the authority, power, and grace shown in Christ's miracles called forth from their recipients and witnesses a judgment as to the identity of the miracle-worker and a response of either love and faith or hatred and murder.

Biblical Miracles Performed By:

Moses	Elijah	Elisha	Jesus

I. Miracles related to natural world

Moses	Elijah	Elisha	Jesus
Ex. 4:3,6-7	1 K. 17:1	2 K. 2:14	Mt. 21:19*
Ex. 7:10, 20, 21*	1 K. 17:14	2 K. 2:21	Mk. 4:39
Ex. 8:6, 17, 21	1 K. 18:38	2 K. 2:24*	Mk. 8:8
Ex. 9:6, 10, 23-25*	1 K. 18:41	2 K. 3:16	Lk. 5:6
Ex. 10:13, 15*	2 K. 1:10*	2 K. 4:5	Jn. 2:9
Ex. 10:22	2 K. 2:8	2 K. 4:41	Jn. 6:5
Ex. 12:29*		2 K. 4:43	Jn. 6:19
Ex. 14:21, 26-28*		2 K. 5:27*	Jn. 21:6
Ex. 15:25		2 K. 6:6	
Ex. 17:6		2 K. 6:18*	
Ex. 17:11*			
Nu. 16:32*			
Nu. 17:8			
Nu. 20:11			
Nu. 21:8			

*miracles causing destruction of life (plants, animals, or people)

Moses	Elijah	Elisha	Jesus

II. Miracles of raising the dead

Moses	Elijah	Elisha	Jesus
	1 K.17 :22	2 K. 4:35	Mt. 9:18
		2 K. 13:21	Lk. 7:11
			Jn. 11:43-44

71

Moses	Elijah	Elisha	Jesus

III. Miracles of healing

Moses	Elijah	Elisha	Jesus
		2 K. 5:10	Mt. 8:3,5
			Mt. 9:2,20, 27
			Mt. 12:10, 15
			Mt. 20:30-34
			Mt. 21:14
			Mk. 1:31
			Mk. 7:33
			Mk. 8:23
			Lk. 13:12-13
			Lk. 14:2-4
			Lk. 17:14
			Lk. 22:51
			Jn. 4:46
			Jn. 5:5
			Jn. 9:7

Moses	Elijah	Elisha	Jesus

IV. Miracles removing evil spirits

Moses	Elijah	Elisha	Jesus
			Mt. 9:32
			Mt. 12:22
			Mt. 15:22-28
			Mt. 17:14-21
			Mk.1:26
			Mk. 5:1

To Think about and Discuss

1. Moses was used by God to perform many mighty miracles in Egypt, many of them bringing destruction to plants, animals, and people. He was expected by God to follow exactly His instructions in carrying these out, and Moses was punished for not doing so in one instance (Numbers 20:7-12). How does this differ from the outcome of Jesus' miracles (with the exception of Matthew 21:19) and the manner in which He performed His miracles?

2. After reading Jesus' statements related to the debate about His miracles from John chapters 5, 10, and 15, how do you understand His explanation of His miraculous works to those who doubted His divinity?

The Created World

In the New Testament, all creation (heaven, earth, and under the earth) was credited to the Christ (Colossians 1:16; John 1:3). Even in the Quran, Jesus is said to have created living beings by breathing in the dust (Sura 3:49). Who else in all history has been able to create from the dust by his breath, other than Elohim, Allah Himself, as recorded in Genesis 2:7 of the Torah? There can not be two different creators.

Even the elements and laws of nature were under Christ's control and could have been used by Him in an attempt to scare or impress people into believing in Him. Satan tempted Christ to demonstrate His power to overcome the law of gravity when he told Christ to throw Himself down from the top of the temple to show how the angels would carry Him and not allow Him to be hurt on the stones below (Matthew 4:5-7). Christ resisted this temptation to use His power in the way Satan dictated, instead we see that the miracles that He performed which related to nature were almost always done to help people who were in need. For example, He ordered the storms and high waves on the sea to be silent because occupants of a boat were about to be drowned. The people still understood that it was a miracle and the surprised witnesses asked one another what kind of person this was that could even calm the wind and sea (Mark 4:41b).

Has anyone ever heard of someone able to walk on top of the high waves of the sea and even command another person to walk on the water, obviously quite deep, without sinking? (Matthew 14:24-33). Who else in the history of any religion could advise professional yet desperate fishermen after a hopeless bankrupt night without a catch, to throw the net in a certain direction to then catch so many fish that they were unable to raise the net? (Luke 5:2-11). No wonder the fishermen left everything and followed Him, Allah's Messiah.

Who is like *Him* who could feed five thousand men, plus women and children, with five loaves of bread and two fish and still have twelve baskets of remains left over? (Mark 6:34-44).

The only other religious leader who performed so many miracles related to the natural world was Moses (as shown in the chart in the previous chapter). It is recorded how Moses, in conjunction with Aaron, followed God's instructions step by step in bringing the plagues upon the country and people of Egypt. These miracles of destruction of life were a direct assault on the ancient Egyptians' beliefs in the false gods and goddesses whom they trusted to safeguard plant, animal, and human life.

● ●

To Think about and Discuss

1. What kind of a truly historical person (not a mythical figure or a movie star) would be able to control the laws that govern nature, as Jesus Christ did?

2. What were there about the conditions of life in Palestine in the first century, and what was there in Jesus Christ's nature that made it possible that the miracles would make up such a large part of Jesus' three-year ministry?

His Miraculous Knowledge

President Abraham Lincoln is said to have commented that it was possible to fool some of the people all of the time and possible to fool all of the people some of the time, but never possible to fool all of the people all of the time. We might add, that it is possible to fool human beings most of the time, but never possible to fool God **at any time!** Who do we think we're fooling, besides ourselves, by pretending to be something we're not? We are minimizing God's greatness and wisdom when we try to pull the wool over His all-seeing eyes.

The Quran says that Allah can see and hear everything (Sura 42:11), and that Isa, Jesus, knew the unseen, "al gheib," (Sura 3:49). Allah in Christ had knowledge of what was unseen to humans, of what was seen and known only by God. He was able to read the minds and hearts of the Jewish religious leaders (Matthew 9:3-4), His disciples, and others around Him, knowing their specific thoughts without their saying a word (Mark 2:6-8).

Jesus' own life experiences as well as His divine nature gave Him insight into the human mind and emotions: "He (Jesus) did not need man's testimony about man, for he knew what was in a man" (John 2:25).

Jesus Christ understood the underlying **defense mechanisms** that people use in their attempt to protect their own sense of personal dignity even if these mechanisms result in great damage to their relationships with others. The Pharisees' use of the mechanisms of *substitution* and *justification* was exposed by Jesus on several occasions. One example is when He uncovered the power-centered selfish interest behind their teachings that allowed men to dishonor parents and give honor and money for religious causes, instead. He confronted them with this question: "Why do you break the command of God (to honor your parents) for the sake of your tradition?" (Matthew 15:3). He knew that many times people try to justify themselves by doing religious acts as substitutes for not living a life pleasing to God. Christ also noted Judas Iscariot's *projection* onto a woman of his own abuse of money. Jesus refuted Judas' attack on the woman's action of taking expensive perfumed ointment with which to anoint Jesus' feet. Judas called it a *waste* and said that it could have been put to better use by being sold and the money given to the poor; and yet it was well known that he was dishonest in handling the disciples' moneybag (John 12:3-8). Yes, even now, it is easy for religious people, even for Christians, to enjoy finding faults in others in order to cover up their own.

The Jewish Pharisees took pride in being descendents of their father, Abraham, and considered themselves acceptable to God because of their strict observance of the religious laws. Yet, Jesus, knowing that even at that moment they were silently plotting His death, told them that instead of Abraham they were really following their father, the devil, who is a liar and murderer, and that they were in need of being released from his bondage of sin. They furiously cried out in *denial* of these accusations, and immediately *projected* their guilt onto Christ, calling Him a "Samaritan" and accusing Him of being demon-possessed (John 8:33-48). Denial is simply conscious or unconscious lying in order to escape the embarrassment or danger of facing reality and admitting the truth.

Jesus understood from His own experience that *rejection* was one of the most hurting and dangerous defense mechanisms used by men. He, Himself, had been rejected by His fellow religious leaders, and even His own family. Yet He never pulled a sword on them in revenge. He noticed and spoke against rejection of the weak (children, women, parents, foreigners, the disabled or ignored) by the strong. Let us examine how Christ compared the eloquent prayer from a self-righteous religious leader and the simple, sincere, spontaneous confession of a man rejected by society. "The Pharisee stood up and prayed about himself: 'God, I thank you that I am not like other men – robbers, evildoers, adulterers – or even like this tax collector. I fast twice a week and give a tenth of all I get.' But the tax collector stood at a distance. He would not even look up to heaven, but beat his breast and said, 'God, have mercy on me, a sinner.' I tell you that this man, rather than the other, went home justified before God. For everyone who exalts himself will be humbled, and he who humbles himself will be exalted" (Luke 18:11-14).

Christ knew that the human feeling of *fear* is a human instinct. One of the phrases He often used in comforting others, was "Don't be afraid." He helped those who feared drowning in the sea and the woman caught in adultery who feared the shame of exposure and the sentence of death by stoning. Jesus relieved them by giving a second chance for both physical and spiritual life to those who had faith in His solution.

The common psychological phenomena of *anxiety* and worry were common among poor people who worried about having enough food and money to take care of their family's needs. Nevertheless, Jesus told them to trust in their Heavenly Father who so faithfully and generously fed the birds and clothed the flowers. Yet there were those who had plenty of material wealth, but were still unnecessarily and unrealistically anxious about collecting more. For example, there was a rich man who had to keep building and filling more and more storage barns in order to feel at peace from his unquenchable paranoia. To him, Jesus gave a warning that he should, because of his imminent death, have a legitimate concern for the state of his soul, instead (Luke 12:18-21).

Ego-centrism and self-love are human inclinations that are very evident in infants and small children which must be nourished and expanded to include the loving of others and ultimately the love of God. Jesus stressed the need for people to develop *self-giving love*, which would motivate them to serve and meet the needs of others. His advice to the rich young man who professed a desire to please God was to sell his possessions, give the proceeds to the poor, come, take up his cross, and follow Him (Jesus). Yet, this youth who had claimed to be seeking an answer as to how he could follow God more closely, went away sorrowfully, unwilling to deny himself the life of ease and pleasure which his riches gave him (Mark 10:17-23).

Jesus looked deeply into *human motives* and encouraged us to have truly pure hearts. He promised that the pure in heart would be blessed because their single-minded vision would allow them to see and understand the priority of God and His will for their lives (Matthew 5:8). Jesus challenged those called by God to follow Him, to leave all things and all people behind. When some gave excuses for postponing their commitment to follow in order to take care of family and business matters first, God revoked their invitations and gave the opportunity to others (Luke 14:17-24). He told the disciple who wanted to go home to say good-bye to those near death, "Follow me, and let the dead bury their own dead" (Matthew 8:22). What a challenging statement by Jesus who knew that He was talking to *ambivalent* followers who needed to make the most important choice of their lives! He reminded them that there would be plenty of worldly people who would take care of the worldly things of this life about which they were concerned.

Jesus Christ knew the background of the strangers He met. Upon meeting a strange woman at the village well within the enemy territory of the Samaritans, the Christ knew her personal history and *underlying needs*. He told her about the six men in her life even though this was the first time He had ever seen or met her (John 4:17-19). When the Jewish teachers of the law and the Pharisees were about to stone an adulterous woman, the only thing that shamed and stopped them from killing her was the Messiah's knowledge and exposure of their own *disguised* sins. This was surely what He was writing in the dust with His fingers in front of each one and what made them shamefully leave the scene upon being told by the Christ that the one who had no sins should be the first to throw a stone at her (John 8:3-11). Christ knew this woman's repentant heart and had mercy for her and her family, and as He instructed her to go and never to repeat her sin, He showed that He was more concerned about a positive change in a sinful woman's behavior than He was in the men's harsh punishment.

In contrast, there is a recorded instance of the prophet of Islam ordering his male followers to kill a confessing repentant adulterous woman after he had given time to make sure that her baby was born and weaned. He is praised for allowing this delay in killing her, but Christ's mercy would have exceeded the baby's weaning! He would have known that the mother's action of coming twice to voluntarily confess, and her truly humble, repentant attitude would be the base for immediate forgiveness. Christ would have spared this valuable life not only for herself but also for the sake of the child's present and future well-being which He knew would depend largely on her nurturing care.

Search the Bible, the Quran, any Hindu, Buddhist, or Confucianist holy book to find a prophet, a religious leader or priest who at any time could know somebody's past and future life and potential, while that unknown person was at an unseen distance. When Jesus met a man called Nathanael, whom He had never physically seen before, He said that this was a true Israelite in whom there was nothing false. When the astonished Nathanael asked, "How do you know me?" Jesus answered, "Before Philip called you, when you were under the fig tree, I saw you." Knowing that Jesus was so far away from physically seeing him and that Jesus had judged correctly his character, Nathanael immediately claimed Jesus as the Son of God (John 1:47-51). Yes, alMasih knows everybody's past, present, and future.

Has anyone ever heard about any person who would foresee his own destiny in detail?! Allah in Christ knew beforehand exactly the time, manner, and place of His future death, and knew the one who would betray Him (John 6:64, 70), calling Judas Iscariot a devil. He knew how long He would be in the grave and how He would rise from the dead (John 2:19-21). Yes, He would be raised by His own power! Quite some time prior to His death, Jesus challenged the few wicked Jewish religious leaders: "Destroy this temple (talking about His body), and in three days I will raise it up" (John 2:19). Who besides Allah's Messiah has ever raised Himself alive, leaving His sealed and guarded tomb after death?! Even the Quran declares that He was "raised to life" (Sura 19:33-34)!

In the New Testament we also see the title, "Word of God," as one of the most important descriptions yet to be given to Jesus, picturing how God communicates about Himself

HIS Word – Kalimatahu – to us is Christ!

through the life and teachings of the Messiah (John 1:1, 14). Christ was the unique and creative Word of Allah (Kalimatahu) as the Quran also claims in Sura 4:171; Sura 3:45; He has the mind and the understanding of God. "In the beginning was the Word and the Word was with God and the Word was *God*" (John 1:1). Christ is the revealing Word that travels beyond space and time from God to man. "In many and various ways God spoke of old to our fathers by the prophets; but in these last days he has spoken to us by a Son, whom he appointed the heir of all things, through whom also he created the world" (Hebrews 1:1-2). As the Living Word from God directed to His children, Christ speaks even in the silence of His actions. He told His critics that even if they didn't believe that He and God were One, they should at least believe that the miraculous works which He did were from God (John. 14:11). Allah Akbar in His Word, the Christ! Is there any other prophet who was or could be described as Kalimatahu (Allah's Word)? No, there is no other one!

All who read Christ's teachings are amazed. He was the most thoughtful speaker ever known in history, putting tremendous meaning, much of it hidden on first glance, behind every word and picture. Because of the limitations of His hearers, Jesus many times used stories and parables that would catch their interest and would be easy to remember and repeat as they were spread from person to person.

Even two thousand years later, who could match Jesus Christ in expressing such thoughtful/comical sayings like, "It is easier for a camel to go through the eye of a needle than for a rich man to enter the Kingdom of God" (Matthew 19:24) or, "You hypocrite, first take the log out of your own eye, and then you will see clearly to take the speck out of your brother's eye!" (Matthew 7:5). How profound His sayings such as, "Even Solomon in all his glory was not arrayed like one of these (flowers of the field)" (Matthew 6:28-29), or "For what would a man profit, if he gains the whole world and looses his life?" (Matthew 16:26)! The Christ knew that some listeners would perhaps understand as they pondered the meaning later, even if not at that moment due to their living in the midst of generalized religious confusion. That is why He gave the parable of the good seed (the message or Word of God) falling on the poor, stony, thorn-choked soil, or on the good soil that brought forth fruit (Luke 8:4-15). He likened those with the fertile receptive soil to those who act on their understanding of the message, and thus bring forth change in their lives. Christ gave His message to all, but He was realistic in challenging them: "He who has ears to hear, let him hear!" (Matthew 11:15). You and I, dear reader, have probably never seen a human being without ears; yet are we honestly recognizing the truth when we *now* hear it? If we recognize it, are we ready to act on it to bring about the changes God desires?

To Think about and Discuss

1. Compare Jesus' astonishing knowledge of the unseen with any Jewish prophet, with the prophet of Islam, and with any present-day religious "prophet" or cult that predicts such things as the exact timing of the end of the world or the second coming of Christ.

2. How do you compare the value of having been exposed to much knowledge, with the value of understanding that knowledge and also being able to use it in a way that brings beneficial results? Read Jesus' story in Matthew 7:24-27 of the opposite results experienced by two different men listening to His wise teaching.

Authority over Jewish Religious Teachings

The Law and Traditions

I grew up in a traditional Christian communty. In the early 1940s the style in which my mother, sisters, and other women dressed for church included only dark-colored, long-sleeved, long-skirted dresses, and head coverings even on the hottest Sunday in August. Through the years, these customs have changed, but modesty and self-respect are still observed. The noted underlying Godly principle was that *modesty* in dress was *one* of the outer signs of an internally pure life. This principle is relevant for all people in all ages in all cultures. Followers of all religions have faced this tension between either following unquestioningly certain cultural and religious traditions or being open to examine their spiritual supra-cultural and timeless relevancy.

Elohim's Moshiach said that He had come to complete the Law and the Prophets, not to destroy them. He had the authority to change and correct portions of the religious interpretations of the law of Moses that promoted a false or inadequate concept from that intended by God. Some may ask the legitimate question, "It is clear that various interpretations (made by men) of the Law can be incorrect, but if the law of

Moses itself came from God, why did it need to be completed by Jesus Christ?"

The term *to complete* means to perfect, to finish, or to bring to maturation. Take the example of the creation by God of human beings. We, as persons, go through various stages growing from conception as a very tiny cluster of cells inside our mother's womb, to a well-formed fetus, to a newborn baby, to a child playing, and to a young woman or man marrying and starting a family as a mature and productive adult in society. Each person has been in an extensive process of completion, perfection, or maturation. Yet, even though we have changed in appearance and developed in our abilities so much, we are still the same person whom God had created and planned us to be from conception. Hidden inside the microscopic fertilized egg was all the genetic material required for the future development and revelation of the human characteristics which were yet unknown to all but God.

Jesus Christ, as the Eternal God in the flesh, had the right to perfect and elevate lower stages of the Law of Moses that were related to the level of development of people at that earlier time in history, to higher stages based on God's original underlying principles. The Christ built upon the laws in the Torah by critiquing their traditional interpretation, explaining their true meaning and applying them to the current situation based on God's unchanging purposes. That is why Jesus emphatically used the expression, "You have heard that it was said…, *But I say unto you…*" (Matthew 5:17-48). For example, Christ said that Moses' law had required men to give their wives a legal document when they divorced them, because before this time men had had the custom of divorcing their wives by just a word of mouth. Divorce was not a part of God's plan for marriage in the beginning when He brought together the one man and the one woman with the instruction that death was the only thing to separate them. However, He had allowed Moses to regulate this evil practice of divorce which had grown out of the hard-hearted, chaotic, relatively lawless, polygamous, and male-dominated society of that time. Christ reminded them that God's original purpose was that marriage was to consist of one man and one woman in a union joined by God, not to be broken by man: "Therefore what God has joined together, let man not separate" (Matthew 19:6).

The Christ also expanded on the underlying spirit of the law relating to adultery: "You have heard that it was said, 'Do not commit adultery.' But I tell you that anyone who looks at a woman lustfully has already committed adultery with her in his heart" (Matthew 5:27-28). Christ went to the core of God's intentions, and warned men not to *blindly* follow traditions handed down by men's interpretations of God's laws. He said to them, "You nullify the word of God for the sake of your tradition" (Matthew 15:6b).

To Think about and Discuss

1. How could Jesus say, "I did not come to destroy the law, but to complete it" and at the same time say, "Moses said…, but I say…"?

2. How did He complete the existing law concerning divorce, murder, and adultery? (Read Matthew, chapter 5.)

3. Give examples of Jesus' practice of not following the letter of the Jewish law, but following the spirit (God's underlying intention) of the law.

Rituals or Relationships?

Why is it easier to follow the principles and guidelines that we have personally noted to be valuable in relating to our acquaintances, than to follow the cold impersonal laws and rules of governmental institutuions such as the IRS or the traffic department? The spirit gives life, but the letter kills.

One of Jesus' main corrections was in regard to the way the most influential Jewish religious leaders were emphasizing outward rituals. They were boasting about their obedience to the letter of the law and tradition, instead of understanding and following the spirit of the law with inner purity and humility in their worship of Elohim (God) and by demonstrating mercy toward others in need or who were not literally following all the traditions. Who else has given such a simple yet so profound principle about religious rituals such as washing the hands, face, and feet before prayer, by illustrating that if you clean the outside of a cup with so much soap and water, and yet the inside is dirty, you still cannot drink from it? (Matthew 23:25-26). Yes, Allah desires a truly repentant heart, clean from the inside, before accepting our ritualistic prayers and fasting.

Who can match the Christ's emphasis on the importance of human relationships over outer acts of worship? He said that "if you are offering your gift at the altar and there remember that your brother has something against you,...first be reconciled to your brother, and then come and offer your gift" (Matthew 5:23-24). He said that if you are unsuccessful in going alone to reconcile with your spiritual brother or sister, you should take with you one or two others from the congregation of the faithful. Try, try, and try again before you leave him completely to God's judgment (Matthew 18:15-17, 21-22). The Christ told us to forgive seventy times seven, that is unlimited forgiveness. But notice that Jesus also indicated that the other person, notably a spiritual brother, needs to give some indication of repentance every time he is to be forgiven. Jesus emphasized that our brother or sister (not our enemy) might need to come to us and "repent seven times in the day" (Luke 17:3-4), and in each of these times, he or she should be forgiven. We hope for repentance and change from spiritual brothers and sisters; otherwise if we ignore their sin, we become enablers and encouragers of evil. It is not only possible, it is even imperative to disagree with sin while still loving the sinner.

Christ loved sinners while feeling compassion for them and wants us to do the same. Can we have this power of love for others who hate us or insult us without change or apology? Can we have the courage to

Are you clean from the inside out?

hate their evil while not insulting back? Let us try. It will bring a change if the persons are open to the power of Allah's Messiah, even if we have to wait a lifetime to see it. When confronted by those who rebuked Christ for fellowshipping with those who were labeled as sinners, he said, "Those who are well have no need of a physician, but those who are sick; I came not to call the righteous, but sinners" (Mark 2:15-17). This love for and mission to help sinners were not only strange and unusual practices for the Jewish religious leaders, they are also quite different from what the Quran teaches. In fact, in it the statement that Allah does not love sinners is repeated.

In their daily lives some Jewish people living in Jesus' day were obliged to come into contact with what was considered *unclean* (e.g., those who touched unclean or dead animals or people, those who were of necessity in close contact with Gentiles, those suffering from certain diseases such as leprosy, and those women who had bloody discharges – monthly menstrual periods, bleeding after childbirth, gynecological diseases. These people were considered *unclean* spiritually and therefore unable to participate in the prayers and other community aspects of worship. They were looked upon with disrespect and as less worthy, just as in some Moslem countries today no woman can enter the place of worship because women are not trusted to comply with the regulation of not entering during a time when they are having vaginal bleeding.

Yet Jesus did not consider such simple, pure-hearted yet downgraded people as unclean and unworthy. He received much criticism from the high society Jewish leaders because His disciples did not follow the traditional hand-washing rules, because He sought out the company of the outcasts, and even went to their homes and ate with them. Christ explained that "there is nothing outside a man which by going into him can defile him; but the things which come out of a man are what defile him. For from within, out of the heart of man, come evil thoughts, fornication, theft, murder, adultery, coveting, wickedness, deceit, licentiousness, envy, slander, pride, foolishness" (Mark 7:18, 20-23). It is interesting that He ended with foolishness (or "ignorance" in other translations). Yes, the intentional and persistent deliberate state of ignorance and unwillingness to learn is sinful. Many of the Jewish leaders, like many people today when confronted by the truths Christ taught, are unwilling to ask God, "Please God, show me the truth." Elohim, Allah, in Christ is willing to open our eyes and remove the blindness of ignorance from our minds and hearts.

To Think about and Discuss

1. Give examples of religious rituals that are practiced today out of tradition without thought about their underlying values and principles.

2. How can we practice the biblical principles of unlimited forgiveness with one who has wronged us while at the same time actively helping the person to change?

3. Explain how the Christian church today should practice the concept of hating sin but loving sinners.

4. Give examples of the difference between someone's unintentional ignorance and his deliberate unwillingness to learn.

True Worship

Our mother had the rare ability to enter into the spirit of worship in many different types of surroundings. She took us to mid-week informal, emotional worship services where interdenominational Christians participated freely, but on Sunday we went back to our more somber regular church service. In the Easter season we occasionally joined the elaborate rituals held in beautiful palm-decorated and candle-lit cathedrals. When she visited us in East Africa, Mother enjoyed fellowshiping and patting her foot in time to their harmonious choirs and enthusiastic African drums. Even though we were worshiping under a large tree and in an **unknown** (to her) tribal tongue, she communicated from her heart with God, through Christ.

The Messiah defied the teachings of the Jewish religious leaders concerning what activities were permitted on the seventh day of rest and worship, called the Sabbath. They judged Christ and tried to prohibit Him from healing on that day, because healing was not one of their allowed Sabbath activities. He disagreed with them and deliberately continued delivering those with demons and curing on the Sabbath those suffering from disabilities and diseases. For Christ, worship was not following a prescribed set of prayers, but was an activity sincerely motivated to bring glory and praise to God. Christ confronted their error in understanding the purpose of the Sabbath by pointing out that while their interpretation permitted the exception of allowing a man to exert a lot of effort on a Sabbath in order to rescue his animal, be it donkey or ox, if it had fallen into a hole, they were not willing to allow Christ to cure sick or possessed people (Luke 14:1-6). He showed them that human beings were of much more value to God than animals and deserved His rescue through the healing of the Messiah, also on the Sabbath (Mark 2:27). He announced that He, Elohim in Christ, had the authority to define what could or could not be done on the holy day (Mark 2:28). He was the Lord of the Sabbath, and those religious leaders could not stop Him, though they tried on several occasions.

For Jesus, a true prayer to God was not just repetition of prescribed words privately, or publicly in order to be observed by others. He emphasized the need for secret and sincere interpersonal communication between each person and God: "And when you pray, do not be like the hypocrites, for they love to pray standing in the synagogues and on the street corners to be seen by men. I tell you the truth, they have received their reward in full. But when you pray, go into your room, close the door and pray to your Father, who is unseen. Then your Father, who sees what is done in secret, will reward you. And when you pray, do not keep on babbling like pagans, for they think they will be heard because of their many words" (Matthew 6:5-7).

For Christ, fasting was not a religious requirement that people must perform as a traditional ritual for all to see and know how obedient they are. He again stressed the *inner* motive: "When you fast, do not look somber as the hypocrites do, for they disfigure their faces to show men they are fasting. I tell you the truth, they have received their reward in full. But when you fast, put oil on your head and wash your face, so that it will not be obvious to men that you are fasting, but only to your Father, who is unseen; and your Father, who sees what is done in secret (unseen by people), will reward you" (Matthew 6:16-18).

The act of gratefully returning to God a portion of what He has given us (whether as tithes, offerings, or gifts to the poor) is a very important part of religious worship, and it came under observation by Christ. He saw the rich people offering much as they entered the Jewish Temple, and He also noticed a destitute widow giving a couple of insignificant coins. As Elohim in the flesh, He knew what was unknown to others: that while the rich had given out of their plenty, what she had given was all that she owned. She was going to leave God's house without a penny in her pocket. But the owner of the universe did not let her leave without a most significant testimony to her act and her motive for worship. He praised her by saying, "This poor widow has put in more than *all.*" (Mark 12:41-44). Yes, more than all others had given, and more than the total of all that was collected, because she out of her extreme poverty had given all that she had. The underlying principles that Christ was stressing were: first, to recognize that all we have belongs to God and secondly, to individually follow His guidance as to its specific use and distribution for God's work, and for our own and others' needs.

How can we compare this teaching with what the rich and famous in Islam and even in some churches and synagogues praise when they say that gathering for ourselves large amounts of honor, power, money, property, and children are the best things in life and proof that God is pleased with us? The Christ tried by all means to diagnose our human greed for accumulating material wealth. He taught that our hearts would be consumed by whatever we treasure most in life, for "where your treasure is, there will your heart be also" (Matthew 6:21). He knew that even with our best intentions to the contrary, material things will take up most of our energy and time in life. He knew that our minds, emotions, and bodies will be over-occupied and overwhelmed by desires, plans, and actions to accumulate, store up, and guard wealth; leaving very little time and energy for following God and His priorities. He saw the conflict in loyalties this would bring and declared: "You cannot serve both God and money" (Matthew 6:24). Our hearts must be kept first of all for selflessly loving and serving God and then secondly for loving our neighbor as ourselves.

Concerning the correct place for worship, Jesus did not argue with the Samaritan woman that she was wrong in worshiping on Mount Gerazim and that true worship must take place in the Temple in Jerusalem (John. 4:19-21). His teaching was that God is actively seeking for true worshipers who will worship Him in spirit and truth (John. 4:23-24). He knew that her concept of God was incomplete and faulty – she was therefore not worshiping Him in truth. He knew that her immoral lifestyle did not exemplify a commitment to draw closely to God – therefore, she was not worshiping Him in spirit.

It is not the position of the body or the geographical location of worship (be it Jerusalem, Mecca, the Vatican, or the Ganges River) that pleases God, but the characteristics and motives of the worshiper which are with him wherever he goes. Many Jewish, Christian, and Moslem pilgrims, some of whom are spending their life savings or even going into debt to travel to one or more of these *holy* sites to *fulfill their religious requirements*, discover sooner or later after returning home that their hearts are unchanged. There may be some culturally motivated outer changes in habits, speech, and dress; but they still lack the inner power that would uproot evil and give them a different quality of spiritual life in the present that lasts forever. Jesus declared it vividly and emphatically — what we need is not a change in outer location (Jerusalem or Mount Gerazim), but a change in the inner location (the heart) in order for us to please God in true worship!

To Think about and Discuss

1. How would Jesus evaluate your revered religious practices of worship such as prayer, fasting, giving offerings, and singing? Are they done to bring feelings of self-satisfaction, as a habitual duty conforming to tradition, or are they done spontaneously?

2. Evaluate the group worship practiced in your church, synagogue, or mosque in the light of the Christ's teachings and attitudes.

Contrast in Religious Leadership

There are all types of leaders. In a recent war, some defeated soldiers gave this reason for losing. They said that their officers upon whom they had depended, sent them into battle with the command: "Forward!" This order was issued from the rear, which allowed the officers to escape in their Jeeps when danger loomed ahead. When the soldiers looked back for guidance, they could not even find their officers. On the contrary, the enemy's officers were the first in line facing danger and their command was: "Follow me!" The enemy soldiers were inspired to fight courageously as they followed their devoted officers. This made the difference in the outcome of the war.

The Christ's authoritative manner of teaching was surprising to those who were accustomed to religious teachers quoting others or referring to teachings (fatwahs) of famous prophets such as Moses. When asked why they had not arrested Jesus, even the officers sent by the Jewish priests answered, "No man ever spoke like this man" (John 7:46). Who like Elohim's Messiah could have the courage to judge, by His own authority, the Jewish religious leaders by telling them directly (not speaking behind their backs) that while at the same time they were lengthening their public prayers, they were eating the poor widows' food (Mark 12:40). He called them blind leaders guiding blind people (Matthew 23:16, 17, 19, 24). Who else could dare criticize the self-righteous religious authorities by telling them that in their false priorities they were straining out a gnat (small insect) while swallowing a camel (Matthew 23:24)? How funny, yet how profound, even to be applied today to some Christians and church leaders who with mixed motives follow pre-conceived ideas and make "quick and easy conclusions" in conformity to others. Instead of objectively searching out the truth of a situation, they make damaging judgments on God-ordained lives, family, church relationships, and or even ministries. Some are simply unaware of the supra cultural biblical principles of relationships and of human psychology. From among the religious leaders judging Christ, only Nicodemus questioned his colleagues' fairness: "Does our law condemn anyone without first hearing him to find out what he is doing?" (John 7:51). Jesus' words are still valid for us Christians who are role-models, especially ministers, lay leaders and church administrators. "In the same way *you judge others*, you will be judged" (Matthew 7:2).

Jesus Christ showed us an everyday model for a godly leader. He said that He came to earth from heaven to serve others, not to be served (Matthew 20:28). He was not coming as the VIP (very important person) that everybody had to bow to; He had compassion for the multitudes whom He described as sheep without a shepherd. He lovingly healed, fed, taught, and counseled; He never used force or coercion. The Christ washed the feet of His disciples and told them to humbly do likewise to others. This was symbolic of true servanthood. Serving each other is not a duty to be performed periodically on prescribed occasions, but is a lifetime of humble sacrificial love in action to others. What kind of a religious leader exemplifies this? Christ's greatness was in His incomparable spirit of servanthood, self-giving, and humility.

Why was Christ so unconcerned about His own rights and position in the eyes of others? He knew who He was and that He had already emptied Himself of His rights when He came from heaven to earth, entering the world to take the form of a servant (Philippians 2:5-8). He was not only willing to humble Himself in life's relationships and circumstances, but was even willing to experience an undeserved death. Not just a simple death where one's heart and breathing stops, but a cruel torturing, shameful public death reserved only for criminals and the worst of society. The innocent Christ was not only willing to give His life, but He received satisfaction and took joy in knowing that He was enduring the severest punishment in our place. We were the ones whose sins deserved the shame and punishment, but He substituted Himself for us: the just for the unjust. He knew that His death would result in the victory over sin, over Satan, and over the fear of death, and that is what He had come to earth to accomplish. Oh, what a uniquely wonderful leader! "Let us fix our eyes on Jesus, the author and perfecter of our faith, who for the joy set before him endured the cross, scorning its shame, and sat down at the right hand of the throne of God" (Hebrews 12:2).

To Think about and Discuss

1. What can today's religious leaders learn from Jesus' example?

2. Have you ever thought of washing the feet (or a similar act of extreme humility) for someone outside your immediate family or in a circumstance other than a planned ceremony or ritual?

3. If you did so, what would be the likely positive and/or negative effects for yourself and for them?

PART IV

"Do What I Do, not Just What I Say!"

How Revolutionary — Jesus' Teaching Concerning Enemies

*A*s a child I had my share of fistfights with schoolmates resulting in several painful injuies, *especially mine*! One time I ran crying to the mother of the bully. She took me inside her home, cleaned the blood from my face, hugged me and asked me to forgive her and her son. She shouted from the door until he appeared. She required that he apologize and tightly held him until he experienced the pain of her hard broom handle. Then she asked, "Now, how do you feel when a stronger person hits you that hard?"

It was impossible for God's Messiah to neglect teaching about and giving examples of the God-like love that Allah wants us to have for others. He knew the importance of relationships in the life of first century Palestine, as well as in all societies in all centuries before and to come. He knew that His own followers as well as Christians down through the ages would be tempted to hate their enemies and even to fight each other. Jesus' teaching known as the Golden Rule states that we should "do unto others as you would have them do unto you" (Matthew 7:12). This is a proactive way of treating others whether they are friends, strangers, or even enemies. It does not mean that we wait to see how they will treat us, and then we react accordingly. It means that we always put ourselves in another's place or shoes beforehand. We should try to imagine how we would feel if our own neck was about to be cut or if we are stripped naked and attacked by a fierce dog just because we differ from our enemy or disagree with his or her ideology. This is still happening in the twenty-first century! Imagine how we would feel if we were in the place of the one we have hurt. Just because he or she is in a vulnerable position or in a state of non-reactive silence out of obedience to Christ, should that encourage us to ignore the situation and become indifferent to the resulting hurt which we have caused?

Many Christians repeatedly or intensely hurt others and then instead of acknowledging the wound and asking forgiveness, are just silent and say, "Let's just forget all about it," or "Why talk about the past?" If they had been badly wounded and were still hurting, would they want to just quietly forget it without a word of apology? Where is their concern and empathy? Many so-called Christians, even within their churches, within their families, between siblings, and even children to their parents or parents to children, are treating others inhumanely. When Christ asks His followers to put themselves in another's place and to feel how they feel, He is bringing us back to our humanity at its best. After all, we are supposed to be different, right? Many Christian leaders, even pastors and missionaries, with all their wonderful gifts of evangelism and preaching, are very poor counselors in trying to assist their members who face these problems. Some leaders are themselves insensitive and hurtful towards others. Some ignore, enable, and/or cover up the obvious evil that comes from those under their influence who are hurting others. Let them stop and think about the Golden Rule before it is too late! If today it is our enemy's turn to be humiliated, tomorrow it may be our turn to be ridiculed. The greatest Judge, Allah's Christ, is watching and everyone, yes, everyone – including Christians – will give an account of their lives at that final Day of Judgment (Romans 14:10, 12). Brothers and sisters and, yes, even Christian leaders, why do we wait for that day when we can apologize and finish with it here and now? If you were the one hurt, you would be helped by an apology; so why leave a wounded person without making amends? If we would all listen and practice this Golden Rule from the Crown Prince of Peace, our families, our neighborhoods, our work places, and also our churches would be much happier and more pleasing to God.

God rains on both: sinner and righteous.

Christ made it clear that God does not love only those who love Him. He loves the sinner and causes the rain and sun to fall on his crops as well as on those of the righteous (Matthew 5:45). His utmost act of undeserving love for man was the loving sacrifice on the cross even for those who did not understand or accept it. The truth is that even while we were sinners, Christ died for the ungodly. We, as God's enemies, did not deserve that God should bruise the Messiah in our stead; yet by His wounds and punishment we were healed and cleared of our guilt (Isaiah 53: 4-6). Allah's Messiah does not love only those who love Him, He loves everyone, yes, all those living within the whole wide world (John 3:16).

Although Christ clearly taught His followers to love one another (John 13:34), He put additional emphasis on loving their enemies (Matthew 5:44). He said that if you love only those who love you, you are no closer to God's requirement and degree of perfection than the non-believers are who also love those who love them in return (Matthew 5:46-48).

Jesus lived in a time when not only the Jews' enemies, the Gentiles, were God's enemies, but even the majority of the Jews themselves, those who had betrayed their God, Elohim, had become God's enemies. The prophet Jeremiah told them: "You distort the words of the living God, the Lord Almighty, our God" (Jeremiah 23:36b), and reported that God was saying to them: "Therefore, I will surely forget you and cast you out of my presence along with the city I gave to you and your fathers. I will bring upon you everlasting disgrace – everlasting shame that will not be forgotten" (Jeremiah 23:39-40). Therefore, the Jews and non-Jews were both alike in the eyes of God; both in need of salvation.

Christ taught that those whom the Jews considered their enemies were really their neighbors and were in the same boat as themselves, in need of love and mercy. He told the story of the good Samaritan (historically an enemy to the Jews), who found a Jew who had been attacked by thugs, robbed, severely wounded, and left to die along the roadside. A Jewish priest and another religious leader had passed uncaringly by the injured man and left him without help. It was only the Samaritan enemy who took his time, stopped, risked his life, gave from his medicine and water, and transported the injured man on his donkey to a place of rest and treatment, financing his care. This Samaritan enemy turned out to be a better neighbor in following Jesus' command to "love your neighbor as yourselves," while the Jewish priest and Levite had acted like enemies towards the wounded Jew (Luke 10:29-37).

The lesson of the good Samaritan was also a tremendous example of Christ's other teaching that we should turn the other cheek to the person who hits us on one cheek (Matthew 5:39). This was in contrast to the Jewish teaching through Moses that an enemy who violently removes or injures an eye or a tooth could be punished in an equally penalizing manner by damaging his eye or his tooth (Matthew 5:38). Before this godly law was instituted through Moses to limit punishment, the retribution being practiced at that time could be the taking of ten teeth for one tooth, or the murder of a man who had destroyed the sight in another's eye, so Moses' law took a long step toward right and fair judgment. Elohim's Moshiach took another huge stride: He made love, not fairness, the rule. The Torah of Moses prohibited indiscriminate or unjustifiable killing; but Christ went even further to teach that we should not even get angry without a righteous cause. Even what we think of as simple insults are sins (Matthew 5:21, 22). In these various historical stages, human life was dignified and elevated from having very little value before Moses, to equal value through Moses, and then to precious value through Christ. If there was ever an example of godly *evolution*, that was it!!

• •

To Think about and Discuss

1. Give three specific examples of how at certain times and situations in your life you have practiced the Golden Rule (doing to others what you would like done to you) in relating to others.

2. Give two specific examples of situations in which you or someone else (keep the person's identity unknown to the group) have ignored the Golden Rule.

3. Reflect on the feelings and effects that resulted with the persons involved in the different types of situations you described above in question 1 and 2.

4. Do the risks of practicing the Golden Rule outweigh the possible positive results?

5. Reflect on Romans 14:10-12 and apply it to today's situations.

6. How did Jesus "evolutionize" the teachings of the Old Testament? Examine Matthew 5:21-22, 38-39; 15:4-6.

Peace or Jihad?

When our fathers spoke of "the war," we all knew they were talking about—World War II. Now when we refer to a certain war that happened in our lifetime, we have to be specific. Was it the Korean War where my brother-in-law fought, the Six Day War during which my wife and I were married, the Yom Kippur War during which our travel time from one country to another took seven days by land instead of the usual four hours by air, the Gulf War, or the Iraq War where my nephew is fighting? As Jesus said: "You will hear of wars and rumors of wars... Nation will rise against nation, and kingdom against kingdom" (Matthew 24:6-7). It is happening in front of our eyes!

When the prophet Isaiah foretold the coming of the Messiah, he called Him the Prince or Head of Peace (Isaiah 9:6). When He was born several hundreds of years later in Bethlehem, the angels came from heaven singing their message that through this joyful event both good will to men and peace were coming to earth (Luke 2:13, 14). Yes, Allah who is Akbar in Christ, the Greatest of *all*, did not need a sword to kill people to force them to accept Him and His teachings. Instead, He sent unarmed angels to proclaim peaceful Jihad (the spreading of God's good news) by heavenly music. Allah's Messiah never raised a sword even in His own defense when He was falsely accused, tried, beaten, and imprisoned. In fact, He even healed the wounds of one of the enemy soldiers who had come to arrest Him (Luke 22:50-51). He had taught His disciples that those who use the sword will die by the sword (Matthew 26:52). Violence brings more violence until it becomes destructive to all, the attacker as well as the one being attacked. The Christ knew that revenge brings only the desire for further and stronger revenge by others even after many years, but peaceful methods will bring peace. That is why He replaced the teaching of the "eye for an eye" with that of "if any one strikes you on the right cheek, turn to him the other also"

Christ felt the sword's edge, but never its handle

(Matthew 5:39). This difficult teaching means that by showing humility, love, and readiness for peace, the good in some men's human nature will, instead of continuing the fight, respond by saying, "If he is giving me the other cheek, let me not take advantage. I will not continue this vicious cycle of violence."

Wars between nations may at times be necessary for self-defense, and for stopping much more violence and the killing of the innocent by tyrants like Hitler, Stalin, and others throughout history — if and where there are no other peaceful means possible. We in America and freedom-loving people throughout the world are indebted to the millions of men and women who fought bravely, were wounded, and some even died in order to ensure freedom for America as well as for other peoples of the world. Without that kind of sacrifice, imagine what the world would be like today. At times, however, if a godly leader is prayerfully and patiently waiting in dependence upon God, he can be given a way out without resorting to war. God will help him distinguish: Is he going into war to avoid much further disastrous consequences not only for his own citizens, but for others unable to defend themselves; or is he making unprayerful, ego-driven decisions for political and/or economic gains? World leaders who are Christians should follow their Prince of Peace. If not, they are simply so-called Christians, who will in the Day of Judgment be told by Christ, "I do not know you."

Why does Allah, Elohim, desire peace? The prophet Ezekiel teaches us that God is not pleased when unrepentant men die either a natural or a violent death, because He knows that only the tortures of hell await them after death. As long as they are alive there is still the chance that they may repent and be changed into pleasers of God who will have a beneficial life for themselves and contribute to the same for others (Ezekiel 18:20-23, 32). God does not enjoy finding faults and mistakes in His creatures. On the contrary, He is "not wanting anyone to perish, but everyone to come to repentance" (2 Peter 3:9). Because of Christ's experience on this earth, He understood so clearly the need for men who live in an evil world to receive the true mercy, *rahmah*, of God.

For Allah's Christ, His struggle was a spiritual Jihad (battle) for righteousness against evil. He struggled against the ignorance and pride of people unwilling to consider any different way of conceiving God than that which was taught them by their ancestors and the traditional religious leaders. This was why Elohim's Moshiach was a much different kind of person. Christ was willing to risk confronting the establishment by His Word, rather than by the sword. He knew that the Word of God is more swift and powerful than any double-edged sword, penetrating to the soul and spirit as it judges the thoughts and attitudes of one's heart (Hebrews 4:12). For the Christ, Jihad meant to struggle against Satan even to the extent of sacrificing His own self for the sake of others — not with bombs and explosives attached to His body that would kill enemies as well as innocent people. On the contrary, He allowed Himself to be put into the hands of His enemies without fighting back. Jesus Christ understood the depth of the pain and suffering of people as His own back and chest were ripped open by the whips of the Roman soldiers, His head cut by the crown of thorns forced through His flesh, His arms pulled out of the joints by the weight of His body as He hung on the cross, His beard plucked out, His hands and feet punctured by nails, His tongue dried by thirst, and His side pierced by the sword. All this was in addition to the humiliation of being spat on, cursed, and looked upon as a blasphemer and enemy of God. Instead of taking other people's lives, He gave His own. In His willingness to die, He was Kabeer, yes, even Akbar! *Larger than Life!* Yes, by His death and victorious resurrection!

Remember, Jesus Christ said that He was the good shepherd who would lay down His life for His sheep. "I lay down my life, that I may take it again. No one takes it from me, but I lay it down of my own accord. I have power to lay it down, and I have power to take it again; this charge have I received from my Father" (John. 10:11, 17-18). This is the practical application of the true *Tasleem* or submission to the will of God which Islam magnifies in theory and in acts of worship. There is no greater love than this, that someone would give (submit) his life for others: not only for his friends, but also for his enemies. Yes, while we were yet sinners, enemies of God, He chose to die for us! We look at the cross and say, "Oh, Allah's Masih, to that extent you have willingly given your life for me!" Allah in Christ's own forgiving example on the cross is unmatchable in all human history. As He suffered, He cried out, "Father forgive them; for they know not what they do" (Luke 23:34). His strength was in sacrificing His own life, *not* the lives of others as in other religions and ideologies. He chose the way of forgiveness, rather than using His fully divine nature to call on more than twelve legions of angels from heaven to destroy all the Jewish and Roman establishments, accusers, and soldiers who were crucifying Him (Matthew 26:53-54).

God, who is Almighty, does not need man's sword to promote His way of life He has already provided His own weapon which is His irresistible self-sacrificing love and forgiveness. Thus, there is no need for further sacrifice of animals in order to please God as celebrated in the Jewish feast of Passover and in the Moslem feast of Adha. The blood of Jesus Christ, the lamb of God, has taken away the sins of the whole world once and for all times, for all those who accept His sacrifice for them on the cross.

Every person who accepts this historical *truth* will not just please God, but will experience a new victorious *life* relationship with Him on a day-to-day basis as this transformed person follows His *way*. He will walk and talk with us, teach, heal, comfort, and protect us – even in the midst of pain, cancer, persecution, imprisonment, and even if we're slashed to pieces – somehow His peace that passes all of our understanding will be our companion and comforter!

To Think about and Discuss

1. How did Jesus exemplify in His life and death the title given Him through the prophet Isaiah, *Prince of Peace*?

2. Are there international situations where wars might be necessary? How might many of them be prevented?

3. Can you ever imagine a situation where the true God, Elohim, Allah, would call upon Christians, Jews, and/or Moslems to fight a *holy war*?

Jerusalem: To Whom Does It Belong?

efore the eruption of this recent phenomenon of violence, churches and synagogues from Australia, the Americas, and Europe used to send thousands of tour groups to visit the *Holy Land*, which, of course, centered around the *Holy City* of Jersalem. While there, they also visited the Wailing Wall and other Jewish sites plus the Dome of the Rock and other Islamic sites. In 1965, my parents took a pilgrimage to Jerusalem and returned with many wonderful stories for us children about their joy in seeing the places where Jesus ministered while on earth. It could be a unifying factor that the three faiths use the same closely related names (Elohim, Allaha, and Allah) and claim the same city of Jerusalem as the location of some of their primary historical holy sites and center for their present day worship. On the contrary, Jerusalem has become a focus of political tension and dispute.

The present day nation of Israel is not to be confused with the ancient Israelites whom God called as His chosen people. After so many attempts to forgive and restore them, it became clear that they as a people continued to break the covenant or pact God had made with them. As a nation they did not become the spiritual blessing to others that God had intended. God had planned that through Abraham's son Isaac *a seed* or descendent would come forth to fulfill the promise that they would be blessed and would become a blessing for the entire world (Genesis 22:16-17). This one seed was the unique person, Jesus of Nazareth (Isa), who in His human nature has descended from Isaac (Galatians 3:16). God said "one seed," not "many seeds," because He knew that the Jewish people as a nation and as a religious system would not accomplish His purpose. This seed, the Christ, came unto His own people (Israel), but was rejected by them (John 1:11). He was crucified outside the city walls of Jerusalem by the plan and decision of His countrymen and the religious leaders who cried out to the Roman governor, "Crucify him! Crucify him!" (Luke 23:20-23) and "His blood be on us and on our children" (Matthew 27:25). This was the ultimate sin: the rejection of their own long-awaited Messiah, because they were unwilling to recognize Him and were more concerned about saving their political/religious system including their place of worship, the temple. And yet their evil plan of sacrificing Christ in order to save their way of life delayed only a few decades the ultimate destruction in 70 A.D. by the Romans of Jerusalem including their Jewish Temple. This destruction had been prophesied by the Christ Himself saying, "O Jerusalem, Jerusalem, killing the prophets and stoning those who are sent to you! ...Behold your house is forsaken and desolate.... Truly, I say to you, there will not be left here one stone upon another, that will not be thrown down" (Matthew 23:37 - 24:2).

The Apostle Paul and other followers of Christ tried to convince their fellow Jews from the Torah, the Writings (including Psalms), and the Prophets that the one they had crucified and who had risen from the dead had been their unrecognized Messiah. When there was little response, Paul turned with the good news of salvation to the non-Jews (Gentiles). Upon seeing the greater response by the Gentiles, Paul and the other disciples realized that anyone from any background who accepted God through Christ did not have to first become a Jew to become a spiritual descendent of Abraham. He said to those believing in Christ, "There is neither Jew nor Greek, there is neither slave nor free, there is neither male nor female; for you are all one in Christ Jesus. And if you are Christ's, then you are Abraham's offspring, heirs according to the promise" (Galatians 3:28-29). These

Will you be a citizen in the new Jerusalem?

new believers in the Messiah (no matter what their background), became known as the new Israel (new people of God), or the new spiritual heavenly Jerusalem (Galatians 4:26; Revelation 21:2).

While they honored the earthly city of Jerusalem in Palestine as a holy historical site, their loyalty and devotion was to the spiritual Jerusalem or Kingdom of God that was being made up of believers in Christ from all generations, cultures, nations, languages, tribes, and yes, from all religious backgrounds! (Revelation 5:9-10; 7:9-10). This new spiritual Jerusalem is not a military or political entity, but is open to all who freely enter by faith, not in slavery to cultural traditions and outward religious rituals as the first Jerusalem had been (Galatians 4:25).

Does this mean that God no longer loves the Jewish people? No, He surely does love them; they were the recipients of much of His love and revelation through the centuries, and the majority of the first believers in Christ were Jews. Throughout history a large number of Jews have believed in the Christ and are now part of the new spiritual Israel. They will live forever as a part of the new spiritual Jerusalem, just as can any person who accepts the salvation available in Elohim Kabeer haMoshiach. "God *so* loved the world (not just one group of people), that he (*so*) gave his one and only Son that *whoever* believes in him… shall have eternal life" (John 3:16). Do the Jewish people still have a place in God's heart and future plans? Yes, the prophet Isaiah (Isaiah 10:20-22; 59:20-21) and the apostle Paul (Romans 9:27; 11:23) taught that a remnant of Israelites will turn from unbelief and sin, come to believe in the Christ, and be saved. Nevertheless, we dare not relate that new spiritual Israel directly to the present political nation of Israel, or the physical city of Jerusalem, both of which today are filled with a large number of people who have no interest in relating personally to or following the Hebrew Elohim or Aramaic Elah (Alaha) of the Old Testament. *Operation World* estimates that the Jews making up the majority of the population in Israel today are composed of only approximately 25% who would be considered "religious" while 75% are secular/humanistic.[17] This makes the present day nation of Israel no more a "truly" Jewish state than America is a "truly" Christian country. They have almost as much pornography (displayed obviously on street-corner newsstands in Jerusalem's Jewish section), immorality, and ungodly behavior and attitudes as the West. Even if the present nation of Israel was faithful to their traditional teachings of the Torah, they would still be in need of accepting the exemplary life and salvation found only in their rejected Messiah. To this day in their relations with the Palestinians, they are still relying on Moses' teaching of equal retribution and sometimes going even to the pre-Moses level of ungodly revenge, destroying homes and many lives of innocent victims. They have pushed thousands of Palestinians away from the homes where they had lived for hundreds of years. At the same time they are still replacing these now destitute Arab refugees with new Israeli settlements and inviting Jews from all over the world to move in instead.

We cannot condone the actions of either the present Zionist Israelis or the present day extremist Arabs, and we do not believe that true Christians can morally support violence to the innocent civilians on either side. Christian churches should not pray for either side to win; we can pray only for the side of righteousness over evil, and for the Just, Fair, and Peaceful God (Allah, al-Adl, al-Muqsit, as-Salam) to intervene so that His will can be known and done. Christians must be sympathetic to millions of Palestinians who have been treated unjustly, denied their basic human rights including that of security, and confined to refugee camps. As much as we condemn (as we should) the anti-Jewish discrimination by Christians including the European Inquisitions, the Nazi holocaust, and the suicide bombing of innocent Israelis by Arabs, we also condemn the Israelis' ill-treatment and killing of innocent children, men, women, and elderly Arabs in Gaza and the West Bank. Christians and other peace loving Moslems, Jews, Hindus, Buddhists – or whoever – need to be equally outraged by Moslem extremists who urge children and youth to blow themselves up in order to kill the innocent civilian Jews in West Jerusalem or Haifa or wherever.

Apart from informative touristic visits to Jewish and/or Christian historical sites, the church in the West is doing very little about peace in the Middle East. The church is largely ignoring the dilemma of both groups of people living in and around Jerusalem in the so-called *Holy Land*. How much are the Christian churches in America praying for God's justice and mercy and applying Christ's teaching of *turning the other cheek* rather than that of *an eye for an eye*?! How do our biases affect the millions of Christians from Arab and Jewish backgrounds living in the Middle East? Are we reaching out even in our own neighborhoods to both or either Jews and Arabs with the love of Elohim, Allah in Christ?

To Think about and Discuss

1. How can the Christian church in the West as well as in the Middle East contribute to peace in the Middle East? (Don't forget, there are about equal numbers of Jews and Moslems (approximately five million each) living in the U.S.A., and more than twenty million people who call themselves Christians living in Middle-Eastern countries made up of either Moslem or Jewish (in Israel only) majorities. Study the figures and the map in chapter 3.

2. What does Jesus offer to both sides (Moslems and Jews) in the Palestinian/Israeli conflict?

3. If you had been born into a family of a minority religious group in one of the countries listed in question 1., what would most likely be the traditional religious faith of your ancestors including your parents? How would that have changed your life?

4. Or if you had been born into a family of a majority religious group in one of those countries, what would most likely be the traditional religious faith of your ancestors including your parents? How would that have changed your life?

How Valuable
Are Children?

*W*hat a wonderful example for our own child who was notoriously restless, to observe the well-behaved and attentive African children sitting quietly during a two to three hour worship service. We also noticed the love and respect which were given these children by their families. Once when preaching at a funeral service outside under the trees, I noted, out of the corner of my eye, three huge cows being herded by a small boy who could not have been over five years of age. Completely naked except for the banana leaf tied around his neck which held his lunch, he was completely in control by the expert use of a small tree branch as he proudly guided these large animals away from the gravesite. What confidence, respect, and love the parents had for this little *man* to entrust him—while they attended the long funeral service—with about fifty percent of their family's livelihood!

Elohim's Moshiach, Jesus of Nazareth, knew what it meant to be the victim of unjustified violence. His parents had to take Him, as a babe, to Egypt to escape being killed among the other innocent children by the Jewish King Herod, who upon hearing that a new king had been born in Bethlehem began to slit their throats.

120

Jesus Christ desired to spend time with children and honored them as shown in His words to the impatient disciples: "Let the little children come to me, and do not hinder them; for the kingdom of God belongs to such as these" (Mark 10:14). He knew they are innocent like the angels, and that what they will become depends largely on what we invest in them and how they are treated. The Christ promoted children's humble attitudes and ability to trust as characteristics also necessary for adults. Once He brought a small child to His disciples and told them that unless they turn and become like one of these children they could not enter heaven (Matthew 18:1-4). Wow! This corresponds to the value He placed on serving others, teaching that in God's estimation the least person could become the greatest or the first, and the greatest become the least or the last (Mark 10:43-45). When one is humble and weak there is

> **For children, Christ was a rock not a stumbling block!**

usually an accompanying openness to look to God for help and less inclination to fight against or resist God's will. When the humble accept God's will in their lives, His power can be more clearly and quickly demonstrated since it is obvious that this power is not coming from themselves. What an unpopular idea then and even now! It is when we are weak and depending on God that we are really strong. His grace is sufficient. His power is made perfect, or is intensified or demonstrated to be useful, when it acts in the vacuum created by our weakness (2 Corinthians 12:9).

What a loss for those who do not recognize the value of children, but abuse their weakness and vulnerability. Those who lead children (or those looking to them for protection and guidance) astray have been promised a severe punishment by the Christ of God. He said that it would be even worse than their being cast into the deep sea while having a stone tied around their necks (Matthew 18:6). What a warning for those also who do not even allow a child designed and created by God to be born! How would anybody think that abortion (including those in late term where the baby is cut into pieces) could be anything less than the murder of an innocent child, one which God *willed* to live?! How would the holy Christ evaluate the thousands of western pornography producers, promoters, directors and adult participants who mislead and ultimately ruin the lives of angelic innocent children? What punishment awaits these throughout the world, especially in the western supposedly "Christian nations" who trample under their feet these beautiful young lives by promoting abuse and prostitution through various means, including the internet?!

How would God judge religious, political and/or military leaders whether in Uganda, Zaire, Sudan, or so-called Christian and rival Moslem militaries in Nigeria who recruit twelve to fifteen-year-old children and teach them to kill with machetes and automatic guns other children, women, or adults from other tribes, just to satisfy the bloodthirsty adults? How would Elohim's Moshiach judge those Zionist leaders in Israel who order the killing of innocent Palestinian children who are simply driven by their need to express themselves by throwing stones against the occupiers' military tanks? These children are being hurt or killed by rubber and live ammunition and helicopter gunships. At the same time, how would Allah (the Most Merciful) justify inciting to violence and even equipping immature twelve to fifteen-year-old Arab children with explosive-filled vests built to rip open their own precious bodies as well as other innocent civilians? Would God justify brainwashed Chechan women who blow up hundreds of innocent school children and themselves, while shouting to the glory of Allah Akbar? All these are grave sins against God, Allah, Elohim. Those motivating, planning, and committing them are held accountable by Him!

• •

To Think about and Discuss

1. Are Christian homes, churches, and schools placing any greater value on children in their actual practices, than those who follow the other religious traditions of Judaism and Islam?

2. If we really place a high value on children as Christ did, what changes will we need to make in our homes, communities, and places of worship?

3. Would you expect nominal Christians to have different values and practices relating to children from those people whom the author describes as "true Christians"? If so, what difference? If not, why not?

Women, Sexual Relations, and Marriage

Respect for Women

*M*ore than any amendment to the constitution or government regulations, the following verse of liberation from the New Testament has done more for women's rights: "There is neither Jew nor Greek, slave nor free, *male nor female*, for you are all one in Christ Jesus" (Galatians 3:28).

The Messiah of God perfected the teaching of the Torah and the traditions of the Jews concerning women, sexual temptation, marriage, and divorce. He honored women not only by words, but by action and attitude. Elohim's Moshiach helped so many women in their different needy circumstances, but never related to them in any physical manner except to heal them. He was concerned about their spiritual condition. He knew that women are not any less spiritually inclined and worthy of religious expression than men. They were not to be treated as "shameful sexual objects" or "a piece of land to be plowed," and to be used for the pleasure of men, as other religions state and teach. The Christ knew that maleness/femaleness has nothing to do with an individual's worth or ability to worship God and be accepted by Him, since we were all created equally (Galatians 3:28).

Once the Jewish teachers tried to trap Jesus (Isa) by asking whose wife she would be in heaven, about a woman who had been the wife of several brothers who had died one after the other. Different from the prophet of Islam who was asked the same question, His answer was that in heaven there would be no marriage or, for that matter, sexual relations, as those who enter there will be as the angels (Matthew 22:23-30) with no need to marry or to relate sexually. Jesus' answer focused on the spiritual fulfillment. The Bible does not give a place for sexual intimacy between men and women in heaven. We will find our greatest fulfillment in heaven as we enjoy the presence and the

> ## Christ lifted women up, not put them down.

awesomeness (Akbarness) of Allah: "Behold the dwelling of God is with (his people). He will dwell with them, and they shall be his people, and God himself will be with them..." (Revelation 21:3). The highest spiritual intimacy will be to see, know, and worship Elohim, Allah, even as we are personally known by Him. Heaven will have an over-abundance of spiritual satisfactions and relationships, not physical. Godly women will be there, not as sexual objects or virgins to be enjoyed by men, but as equally precious souls having the same place and rewards as those of the righteous men. In contrast to Islamic teachings, women are exactly equal spiritually to men, are not deficient in mind and religion, and are not predicted to be the majority of hell's inhabitants.

Jesus Christ taught that heaven is a kingdom where those belonging to the King (God) will dwell together with the King, and where His will is done: "For the kingdom of God does not mean food and drink (anything physical) but righteousness and peace and joy in the Holy Spirit" (Romans 14:17). Surely if Allah is Almighty (Akbar), King (al-Malik), and Possessor of the Kingdom (Malik al-Mulk), He is able to provide sufficient spiritual satisfaction in heaven without needing to resort to earthly physical satisfactions to please men. Even the wildest dreams of man that he might be satisfied by such things as comfortable couches, dozens of virgins, food, cool shade, wine, and other physical comforts, are less than a drop in an ocean compared to the spiritual satisfaction that God has planned for us in heaven. It is not right to picture a type of heaven to please our own human imaginations and desires, for it is written, "'What no eye has seen, nor ear heard, nor the heart of man conceived, what God has prepared for those who love him'" (1 Corinthians 2:9). If some people feel that they would not have enough happiness in any place where the only thing to enjoy is Elohim Kabeer, Allah Akbar, then they should ask themselves if they really know and appreciate Him in His fullness.

To Think about and Discuss

1. What are some of the discriminatory acts, attitudes, and double standards that people from the various religious backgrounds practice in relation to women?

2. The author believes that the Bible teaches that sexual relations and gratification will not be found in heaven. Do you find a differing view in the Bible? If not, what will there be in heaven to replace sexual satisfaction for both men and women?

Sexual Temptation

Why are women to be viewed as irresistible symbols of sinful sexual temptation that need to be covered from head to foot or veiled in order to protect the "assumed to be innocently weak and vulnerable" men? Poor Men! This paints a picture that man has no self or God-given control over his own mind, will, and body. Certainly women should not be shamelessly exposing themselves as we see some of them in western movies and television. They should be modestly dressed and well-behaved for their own self-respect and in order not to draw man's sexual desires to their bodies. In contrast, Christ directed His teaching on temptation to the men. He knew that in every society, including the so-called Christian West, in reality many more men will be committing adultery with a much smaller number of women and prostitutes. He knew that it was usually men who were seducing young girls and raping women, and much less frequently the opposite. He tried to make the point that men, as the leaders and most powerful members of society as well as the heads of their families, should take the responsibility for guarding their own thoughts and actions and become the protectors of women. He told them that if they even looked lustfully at a woman, they had already committed adultery in their hearts (Matthew 5:28). Christ didn't blame the woman if she did not completely cover herself with long robes and veils, but instead directed His criticism to the man, advising that if his eye tempts him to lust, it would be better to take out that eye and go to heaven half-blind than to let his eye lead him to sin (Matthew 5:29). What a powerfully meaningful way to teach men, whom He knew to be the ones having the most lustful eyes and thoughts, whether a woman was veiled or unveiled. Let us be honest, how often are men not only unveiling but even stripping women by their wicked eyes in the streets and in places of work, while at the same time ordering their own wives, sisters, daughters, and even mothers to be veiled? Men may try to cover their sin by false piety, repeated prayers, fasting, and quoting religious verses, but God knows better. These religious practices mean that they believe that God is closing His eyes in the face of their sins. Where is the emphasis on the purity of the heart, motives, and actions that the Messiah taught was so important to God?

Haven't we also heard about and seen promiscuous women and prostitutes who are dressed modestly or even veiled? Have we noticed the veiled women who spend thousands of dollars for perfume and plastic and other surgeries to make their bodies more attractive to men? Haven't we also heard about and seen unveiled, decently dressed women and girls who are much cleaner morally in front of God and society? It is not the outer appearance that guarantees protection against sin. The best guard against becoming a sexual temptation for others and against being ourselves tempted, is a God-given spiritual power. Only by accepting the crucified and resurrected Christ as our personal Savior, can we receive the necessary overcoming inner power from God which enables us to be victorious over sin and Satan.

To Think about and Discuss

1. How do the teachings of Allah in Christ and Allah in Islam differ in how they view a man's responsibility in relation to sexual temptation?

2. What is a woman's responsibility in the area of tempting men and in being tempted herself?

3. In what practical ways can we start applying Jesus' teachings related to sexual temptation as we raise our children?

Marriage

My new wedding certificate was thrown as trash out the window of the governmental headquarters by the enemy forces taking over the country one week after we were married. Being too preoccupied with post-war circumstances and responsibilities, there was no time to wonder if we were officially married or not. Some seven months later, a friend brought a wrinkled paper which he said a shopkeeper had wrapped around his purchase of feta cheese. When removing the cheese, my friend looked more closely and found my name on the paper! **Here was my stinking notarized wedding certificate!** Had we been legally married all this time or not? Yes, we always were. Since God had put us together, no war, no government, no trash, no feta cheese, would separate us!

Jesus, the Master Teacher, referred back to the original purpose of God for marriage when He created one Eve to marry one Adam (Matthew 19:4-5; Genesis 2:21-24). To have more than one woman for one man whether under the label of "polygamous marriage," "trial marriage," "temporary marriage," "girlfriend," "an affair," "pleasure marriage," "common law marriage," or "fornication before marriage," is simply *wrong*. Christ repeated what God had ordained from the time of Adam and Eve: that the *two* became *one* — one physical, social, mental and spiritual union — in one home. Children need one faithful set of parents, not multiple confusion. One man and two, three, or four women; or one woman and two, three, or four men cannot become *one*. They become two or three or four sets of confusing unions, … period! Only 1 x 1 = 1 (one union). 1 x 2 = two sets of unions and 1 x 4 = 4 sets of unions. There is no way to guarantee justice or true harmony among two, three or four sets of couples, nor to avoid endless jealousy and conflicts. It is clear and simple with no justifications, no mitigating circumstances. The few situations of polygamy in the Bible do not justify that practice, but only give us examples of what was happening in early human history and show the consequences of disobeying God's strict command of one husband for one wife. Look at the unbelievable problems that resulted from having more than one wife and more than one set of children, from the examples Abraham, Jacob, David, Solomon, and others. These acts of polygamy were all committed against God's plan, direction, and will; and all ended with terrible consequences of break-ups and break-downs for the parents, the children, the descendents, and the Israeli nation as a whole. Look even today at the broken homes that have resulted in the destitution and prostitution of women, as well as millions of children with deep hatred and jealousy towards their siblings from different mothers with the same father, or different fathers with the same mother.

Allah's Masih said that what God has united in marriage should not be separated by man (Matthew 19:4-6). A man who marries has to be ready to live with his wife (and she with him), regardless of the circumstances, until the death of one of them. God in Christ does not sanction the practice of nominal Christians or Jewish men and women living together before or instead of marriage as is often and increasingly seen in the West, or an actual marriage officiated in a Christian church or Jewish synagogue that is quickly and easily dishonored by "affairs," socially accepted adultery, or divorce. The cheap "no fault" divorces that are promoted by nominal Christian and Jewish lawyers and accepted in the West are equally saddening to the God who says, "I hate divorce…" (Malachi 2:16). Failing to keep one's commitment to the marriage partner because of a simple disagreement over the color of one's automobile, taking up more than one half of the bed, cutting one's hair without permission from the spouse, or even a much more serious reason is falling far short of God's plan and standard!

There is no justification for a man under any circumstances, except adultery of the spouse, to be ready enough to simply say "You are divorced" to his wife and mother of his children, or even if she has no children. Who can imagine that under the umbrella of a "religious law," man could put the one whom God, Elohim, Allah, had joined to him into such a stressful situation, and perhaps push her towards sin in order to meet her and the children's needs? It is taught in Islam that a husband can divorce his wife by repeating three times, "I divorce you." After that she cannot return; they cannot live together as husband and wife. Even if he was only nervously over-reacting in a moment of anger, the third time he says "I divorce you," he can only bring her back by following another "religious law." This Islamic law requires a divorced woman to marry a second man (Al Mohalil - the legalizer) with the assurance that they have sexual relations before this temporary marriage can be terminated (Sura 2:230). Only then, can she return to the fellowship of her children and her life-long husband by remarrying him. How would her innocent children feel when they notice their mother's humiliation by this second artificial husband, who could be in reality a temporary sexual master forcing her against her will into a longer and longer time for sex before releasing her to return to her beloved but weak, mistaken, estranged husband who is their father? Would Allah's Christ have sanctioned such a habitual divorce and the sleeping with an artificial husband to establish a family lifestyle pleasing to a pure, Holy God? By no means would Allah correct one mistake by another mistake!

Any sexual union outside of marriage or the adding to the one living, legal wife, be it for pleasure, for bringing children, or for whatever purpose, is simply against the will of Allah. Yet some men say that his (man's) will is that his needs must be met, whether it is the need for children, the needs fueled by sexual lust, or the need for more family members to administer property, or by mixed motives. Why do we say that Allah does what He wishes, and then fight against it by doing our own will? Two of the most common phrases used by religious persons are "Insha'Allah," meaning "if God wills," and "Al Hamd le'Allah ala kul hal," meaning "thank God for all conditions." The person using these terms sounds very submitted (*Musalem*) to God's will, and yet in practice many times he is not willing to submit if it goes against his own personal will. That means that in truth, he is not thanking God for every condition. For example, a person may say that the barrenness of his wife is God's will and yet he may divorce her or take a second wife to overcome the consequences of that barrenness. Yet, if the inability to have children lies with the husband and not with the wife, does the wife have the right to take another husband in order to fulfill her need to have children? Or is she considered to be the one to submit and be content and to say it is God's will for her to never be a mother, but only for him to be a father? The second option is what is taking place. Men, wake up to these injustices and inconsistencies! Is it not possible for a man to consider his invalid wife as God's will for him, necessitating him to stick with her in thick and thin, just as she is required to do if he is the sick person? Why would a rich man be able to marry more than one wife, while the poor man is not able? Does God have a different will or rule for the rich than for the poor, for the man different than for the woman? Are the women to be penalized, while the men are allowed to be pleased with sex with other women? Does the husband's handsomeness, money, or sexual ability to enjoy three or four wives allow each of the co-wives to experience that special relationship that God intended when only two persons share their minds, bodies, and souls in the unique way that He called "becoming one flesh?" Only one husband and one wife, with no extra partners whether they be co-wives or adulterous persons, can become *one* in a holy lasting marriage. Yes, God has created us to be in His own image, which is much different from animals.

* *

To Think about and Discuss

1. Examine whether Abraham's and King David's polygamous family relations were following God's plan. What were the results experienced by them, their wives, their children, and their descendents?

2. Give examples from our societies today about how sharing the bed with more than one spouse/non-spouse has affected children and family relationships.

3. How fair and beneficial to all family members involved (the husband, the wife, the children) is the Islamic law that allows men to divorce women just by saying certain words, and the law prevalent in parts of the Christian West that allows quick and easy "no fault" divorces?

4. How do you compare divorce practices before Moses, divorce according to Moses' law, and the divorce practices mentioned in question 3., with the teachings of Jesus?

Homosexuality

What a shock to all true Christians throughout the world when the national hierarchical leaders of a certain large Christian denomination in the West recently decided to ordain a practicing homosexual as their bishop. Their constituents in Africa have courageously questioned their association with this mother church because of such an unbiblical practice.

The present upsurge in homosexuality in nominal Christian nations makes it no more acceptable than it was in the days of Abraham's nephew, Lot, when he lived in Sodom (Genesis 19:4-25). Nowhere in the Bible was homosexuality (sexual relations between two men or between two women) accepted or condoned. In fact there is quite clear teaching against it (Romans 1:26-27, 32). Homosexuals need to repent, change, and be saved in the same way as any other sinner. This does not mean that persons practicing homosexuality should not be loved unconditionally. Allah's Christ died for them as well as for the rest of us sinners. Thank God, there are several Christian ministries that are demonstrating the "tough love" of God in reaching out to homosexuals and helping them to change their lives, by the grace and power of God. They need the love and support of *true* Christians, just as any other victim recovering from sin's consequences.

However, for Christian churches or pastors or priests who practice, condone, or promote homosexuality as God's will, it is a terrible blasphemous ignorance of God in Christ, the Judge, who will tell them if they persist in this evil up to the Day of Judgment, "I never knew you...[Get] away from me ... [to] be thrown into hell where 'their worm does not die, and the fire is not quenched'" (Matthew 7:23, Mark 9:47-48). Yes, God's judgment and eternal death is awaiting all unrepentant sinners, no matter if their sin is sexual in nature or not. Please, Church of Jesus Christ, weed any known sin from your midst; otherwise God's anger will be upon those who also condone it or even tolerate it! Sin is sin...period... and it is even worse when it is found in the religious leaders who are to be held more accountable because they become stumbling blocks for others. Christ's words are for me and you: "From whom much is given, much is required" (Luke 12:28). To so-called Christian pastors, presbyters, lay leaders, bishops, and archbishops who practice, condone, or even are silent about homosexuality, sexual abuse of children, adultery, easy divorce, wife abuse, discrimination against women, or any other immoral, unethical act: God's word now is "Repent, before it is too late!" Otherwise His judgment in eternity awaits. As He said to the Jewish religious leaders, He will say to them, "You stood in the way for people to enter the Kingdom of Heaven. Neither you entered... nor you allowed others to enter" (Matthew 23:13). God in Christ is Almighty, Great is His judgment!

To Think about and Discuss

1. Starting with creation and continuing through the last book of the Bible, what are the scriptural principles related to gender?

2. What is the impact on children, schools, the work place, and society as a whole when God's natural laws and biblical standards related to sexuality are broken?

3. What are the distinctively disastrous results when Christian leaders and/or churches ignore, condone and/or practice homosexuality?

PART V

Humans: Our Own Best Friends or Worst Enemies

Nominal Christians and Nominal Christian Societies

*O*ne of the most influential books that peaked my interest in cross-cultural perception was *The Ugly American* which demonstrated how even one U.S. citizen can color people's judgments for or against a whole nation. A similar book I would call *The Ugly Christian* is daily being written in the minds of many people from other parts of the world as they are closely observing those whom they believe to be Christians.

America, Europe, and now much of the western influenced societies in Latin America, Australia, and other countries are plagued by an overt array of lawlessness, immorality, and unethical conduct. We could say these conditions are anti-Christian, anti-Jewish, anti-Islam, and anti any other religious system that believes by some degree in the Holiness of God and His requirement for a pure lifestyle for His followers.

Industrial and technical advancements of the West, combined with its available capital, have allowed countries that have been historically Christian to be the source of material generosity as well as promoters of honesty, freedom, and goodwill to the rest of the world. Now, as their citizens have drifted away from their religious roots and have become more and more materialistic and pleasure-centered, they have on the contrary become the countries who are known to be the slaves to and sources for pornographic films and television, alcoholic beverages, profanity, and anti-God philosophies for the remainder of the world. The so-called Christian nations such as America are experiencing a great moral decline with increasing crime, drug and alcohol addiction, infidelity between husbands and wives, pregnancies among unmarried girls, and sexually transmitted diseases. Many people in the world do not realize that although America was founded by a people the majority of whom were deeply committed to God, the succeeding generations have become more and more secularized. Many Africans, Arabs, and Moslems still think that all of America's people, the government, politics, and the military represent Christ just because we were historically a Christian nation. While we might wish that to be so, and there are no doubt "true" Christians to be found in each of these arenas, this generalization is certainly false today. This is difficult to comprehend for people who equate one's religious affiliation with one's culture. In Islam, once you are born to a Moslem father, you automatically become a Moslem. There is little question or choice for anyone born in that religious culture to have any other beliefs different from that of their parents, extended family, and clan. However, in a country with freedom of religion, it is possible to have many different religious groups functioning in the same community, and even represented in the same family. What has happened is that freedom to choose also means freedom to not accept or even to reject. This is especially obvious as one recognizes that there are those who are just cultural or nominal (in name only) Christians. They are to be differentiated from those who have actively and intentionally chosen to relate to God through Jesus Christ with a personal faith and commitment, whom we call *true* Christians.

To be born to Christian parents, with Christian-sounding names, from a so-called Christian heritage such as in a country that calls itself: "one nation under God," does not make one a "true" Christian, one whose goal is to please God in all aspects of life, including thoughts, attitudes, actions, morals, and ethics. Many Christians do not practice Christ's concern for others. Living in an individualistic world, they disregard spouses, family members, neighbors, and others. The world watches the violence in "Christian" America as sick family members are eliminated, youth kill each other in their schools, and children are raised on violent cartoons and video games. It has been estimated that sixty percent of those who are designated as "Christians" in the world today are Christians in name only, and are in actuality non-practicing Christians.[18] They do not know that while it is possible to be a non-practicing *religionist*, it is impossible to be truly a *non-practicing Christian*. The very definition of a *true* Christian is one who has an active personal faith in God, has truly repented from sin, and trusts the finished work of Christ for salvation. This person realizes that his/her body is the dwelling place or *temple* of the Spirit of the living God. His Spirit is holy and seeks to purify the life of the person who surrenders to live in harmony with the Spirit's directions, refusing to live according to self-centered desires. This person is enabled by God to exemplify truth, honesty, straight-forward relationships, concern, and respect for others in speech and actions. This lover of God follows the example of his Savior in praying for God's will, not his own, to be done in every area of life, and spends his time and resources in sharing God's mission of loving outreach and service to the world. The *true* Christian also honors his body, which now belongs to God, by not allowing sexual immorality or abuse of drugs (whether over-the-counter, prescription, cocaine, marijuana, hashish, kaat), cigarettes, or alcohol which dishonor the Creator and destroy the body which He has created to be healthy, productive, and useful for God's service. The lives ruined, including those of innocent victims, the false religious picture being promoted, and the billions of dollars and other resources being spent and wasted by so-called Christian nations on these abuses is an offence to God the Creator, and to the name of Jesus, His Messiah. These false pictures of Christianity must be exposed by "true" Christians for what they are: *Sin*, and a renewed effort must be made to evangelize these lost brothers and sisters.

When such ungodly, heinous acts like the inhuman mistreatment of the Iraqi prisoners of war by the American military are committed, American Christianity is perceived, especially by the Arabic and Islamic worlds of over a billion persons, as being a perverted religion and society. Swift and severe punishment must be meted out in a public manner to those responsible for such evil acts. The government and military personnel need to be held accountable so that no one feels he is above or out of reach of the long arm of the law. There, furthermore, is no room for making mistakes in conflicts and risking innocent blood being shed under a blanket that is labeled as "unavoidable collateral damage." Deep apologies from all those who are responsible for such acts, and the highest possible compensations are absolutely necessary. Human blood is not cheap, and more than excuses must be given when it is spilled. The church of Christ should be among the first to condemn these acts and demand severe punishment for those (on all responsible levels) who did them or allowed them to be done. The Christian church needs to act as the conscience for the so-called Christian West, or what, sadly, is considered by a large section of the world as the *wild, wild* West. Sad to say, many times the church is not doing what Jesus Christ requires of it.

Another blight upon the name of Christianity is the in-fighting that goes on between different Christian groups and denominations, and between Christians and members of other religions. Some of the most odious of these throughout history have been the Spanish Inquisition, the Catholic-Protestant wars, and the Crusades. Almighty God's Messiah would never condone hatred, injuring, bombing, imprisoning, or killing from anyone in any group (called by His name or not), apart from clear self-defense, or in prevention of the destruction of others. Did God in Christ motivate the hatred and killings involved in the so-called Christian Crusades of the eleventh, twelfth, and thirteenth centuries? Absolutely not! God does not contradict Himself; He is not both love and hatred. He is either one or the other, and it is clear that He is *love*. The Crusaders had the right to liberate only their own European lands, but they had no God-given authority to use the cross along with the sword to invade Islamic countries and kill Moslems to liberate Jerusalem. Only tremendous enmity has resulted from that very anti-Christ-like brutality. The shedding of blood can only bring more blood, and in war it is not only soldiers who are wounded and die, but many innocent people. Why would innocent Moslem widows and orphans have to suffer? Why didn't the Crusaders apply their Christ's Golden Rule – doing only what they would do if there were innocent

Christian or Jewish women and children involved? Allah's Masih would never accept that His followers use the sword in one hand and the cross in the other in such a context.

For people who read this book who are not from a Christian background, please understand. If you try to follow the example of many nominal Christians, you will be greatly disappointed and even caused to stumble in your search for truth. Sad to say, you might see a Christian person, leader, and even minister or priest hatefully insulting others, committing adultery, cheating, lying, justifying, or covering up for others' sins. If you

Don't loose sight of Christ or you'll get lost!

see these, turn away in pity and then remember to look only at the Messiah, our perfect example. "Let us fix our eyes on *Jesus*, the author and perfector of our faith" (Hebrews 12:2). This does not mean that there are not many honest, faithful Christians and Christian leaders who, while they might sin, come back to their Lord on their knees and repent deeply from their hearts. They receive His forgiveness and by the power of His Holy Spirit are enabled to overcome the power of temptation and to live a victorious life over habitual sin. This great Spirit, which is the same one who raised Christ from the dead, is able to raise up His followers to walk in a new life that is changed from the old, and is eternal (Romans 8:11). In short, it is essential for the one honestly searching for God to look at Christ, not at individual Christians, or to the church, or to Christianity as a whole. As Christians, we may surely disappoint you, but Allah's Christ will never, never disappoint you.

To Think about and Discuss

1. How necessary is it for adherents of the various religions to evaluate and self-criticize their own beliefs and practices?

2. Identify some of the unique teachings of Christ that are in conflict with some of the practices of individuals who call themselves Christians and the so-called Christian countries?

3. What do *true* Christians need to do to make it easier for the world to believe the message of Christ?

4. If you are from another religious background, what is the least attractive thing you have noted about so-called Christians and Christian nations?

5. Have you ever met someone whom the author might describe as a *true* Christian?

Does Elohim, God, Allah, Need Man's Military or Terroristic Assistance?

*O*ut of gratitude for what God Almighty does for us, we sometimes want to assist Him with what we believe to be His causes. If done in the right context under His direction, this is appreciated and encouraged; but in other contexts, God has His own will and means which He reserves only for Himself. If we're not careful, we can overstep the boundaries, bringing harm to God's cause, others, and even to ourselves. An unwise expression of gratefulness was exemplified by the man carrying a heavy load of wood on his back. A sympathetic truck driver stopped to give him a free ride in the back of his truck to his distant destination. When the driver looked through the back window, he found that his passenger was standing with the heavy load still tied to his back. The driver stopped and asked, "Why don't you put your load down and rest? That's why I stopped to give you a ride." "Oh, kind sir, you were so good to carry me, I wanted to do my part and *relieve you* from some of the load," was the man's grateful response.

God is the only self-sufficient being in, beneath, behind, and beyond the world. He does not need us to protect Him or to stand in His place of judgment on others. He is the *Almighty*. Yet, throughout history men have been challenged to stand true to their beliefs in God and give verbal defense for their faith. The result of this defense for many has been ridicule, discrimination, persecution, and/or death; and strangely enough this persecution is done by those who believe they must offensively attack anyone with a differing faith in God. We see this is what happened with Stephen, the first Christian martyr (Acts 6:8-8:3) who was stoned to death by religious Jews, including Saul who later became the apostle Paul, who believed Stephen was denigrating their beliefs. Yes, there have always been those people who think they need to fight on

God desires testimony not torture!

God's behalf, to punish those whom they believe are blaspheming God, the Holy Writings, or His prophets. The Christ even prophesied that His followers would be persecuted by those who would think they were doing God a service (John. 16:2b). There is a very clear dividing line between honoring, respecting, worshiping, and giving testimony about Elohim, Allah, God Almighty, even when we know to do so will bring persecution, and between brutally attacking others through means that He Himself does not approve of in our attempt to defend Him, His reputation, or His name. We have already decried the Crusades, where Christians tried to re-capture their holy sites in Jerusalem by military means, killing innocent people in the process.

In the ancient history of the Israelites their most holy religious symbol, the Ark of the Covenant, was stolen by enemies and taken into enemy territory. The Ark symbolized God's teachings, the Ten Commandments, as well as the site where God was to meet with man in worship. This was a terrible loss in terms of their religious practices, as well as a blow to the pride and national identity of the Israelites. When the enemies placed the Ark in the same room with their idol god, Dagon, the idol fell on its face and was broken. The enemies also began experiencing various diseases and negative happenings until they, themselves, realized that they had offended the awesome God of Israel and needed to return the Ark to its proper place. When finally the Ark was returned, it was not recovered by means of the might and force of the Israelite army. The Almighty God did not need the Israelites to avenge the enemies who had done this evil. Elohim was great enough to work on His own behalf to punish the enemies and to demonstrate His spiritual power in causing the Ark to be returned. He brought glory to His Name rather than to the military power of His followers (1 Samuel, chapters 5 and 6). Even when the jubilant Israelites, upon receiving the returned Ark, opened it to look inside (something strictly forbidden by the law of Moses), they were struck down dead! What a demonstration of God's power and holiness given to both enemies and children of Almighty God that would never have been seen if the Israelites had rushed off to try to avenge Jehovah on their own! This is a lesson from which we can all learn in order to help all three groups: Jewish Zionists, Moslem extremists, and even the few Christian radicals who believe that they are carrying out God's desires or fulfilling His promises, even if that means the killing of others.

If Allah is really Akbar, He can and will make His own retribution if and when His own character and glory have been violated. "Beloved, never avenge yourselves, but leave it to the wrath of God; for it is written, 'Vengeance is mine, I will repay, says the Lord"' (Romans 12:19 quoting Leviticus 19:18; Deuteronomy 32:35). In fact, God the Avenger, (al-Muntaqim), is the only One able to repay in a wise and just way, since He is the only One who knows people's hearts and therefore, the only One who knows who is really guilty, who are the evil planners and who are only the ignorant followers. He is the only One able to choose the suitable means with which to repay, and the correct timing so as to be most meaningful to those being punished and those who are witnesses.

Does this say something also to Christians and so-called Christians who do not see the line that separates the following actions:

... the hunting down of criminals who are committed to destroying you or others in acts of terrorism such as was experienced on September 11, 2001,

... the indiscriminate killing of a bearded Moslem person in one of the cities of America, a look of hatred towards a veiled girl, or a word of anti-Jewish ridicule?

Allah in Christ will never condone any deliberate injustice from any source.

To Think about and Discuss

1. Can you remember other biblical events where the Israelites tried to move militarily without God's direction? And from more recent history where religious people have tried to seek vengeance on behalf of God? What were the results in each instance?

2. What do Christ's teaching and example of loving our enemies have to say to Jewish Zionists, Moslem radicals, and the extremely militaristic Christians in terms of persecuting and/or waging a "holy" war against those from different religions whom they consider to be enemies of God or of God's promises?

3. What are some "non-Christ-like" attitudes or actions by "true" Christians that demonstrate a lack of love, or even antagonism towards others? How can these be changed?

Is God Behind Our Discrimination and Prejudice?

*H*ave you ever experienced firsthand the pain, shame, and anger that comes from discrimination? You may say, "I have never treated anyone badly because of their skin color." Maybe not; but have you ever lost patience and become irritated with the person at the counter, on the phone, or the taxi-driver whose broken English and mispronounced words, or complexity of expression slow you down? There are all kinds of prejudice, and even among the most religiously devout leaders!

Throughout many parts of the world regardless of the dominant religion, people seem to have an ungodly preference for light-colored skin, with a resultant discrimination of varying degrees against those having darker skin. This discrimination is perhaps more pronounced among people having lighter skin themselves, but it has also been noted among all intermediate and darker shades as well, even to the extent of making the darkest ones slaves to those of the medium shade.

There is no teaching in the Bible that would say that Elohim, God, values or de-values people on the basis of their physical bodily characteristics. In fact, God's emphasis is on men's motives, attitudes, and actions which arise out of their internal values and in response to the character and works of God. The most well-known biblical teaching is the one given by Jehovah to the prophet Samuel who was trying to choose a king by observing the more attractive looks and superior demeanor of one of the brothers of David (who was the one to be chosen by God). God told Samuel, "Do not look on his appearance or on the height of his stature … for the Lord sees not as man sees; man looks on the outward appearance, but the Lord looks on the heart" (1 Samuel 16:7).

Some people have tried to say that Christianity is the white man's religion; yet Jesus (Isa) was a first century person of Jewish background, which means that he was probably of medium to dark brown skin tone. Although Jesus, the Messiah, has been portrayed by Western artists as having light skin and blue eyes, there is no reason to think that to be true any

Christ is not colorless, but colorful!

more than the African artists' portrayals that He had dark black skin with Negroid features, or the Oriental paintings of Him having oval eyes. To every person, the Messiah has been felt to be one like them. His human appearance should not be an issue. Some people have considered Him "the colorless Christ," meaning that He was color-blind when looking at people. I prefer to call Him "the colorful Christ," because of the variety and blend of peoples to whom He showed love and concern, as well as respect for each unique culture.

Jesus Christ valued all people with no consideration of skin color. We wish we could say the same for His followers. One of the grave sins in history committed by the majority of whites throughout Europe and America who happened to have been nominal Christians is slavery of black persons coming from Africa, and the discrimination against the native Indians of North and Latin America. That those who say they follow Christ could practice such a sinful inhuman system of slavery and racial discrimination is shameful. Churches and true Christians who follow the teachings of Christ have been trying, and should do even more today, to correct the results of these evils and to work for equality in all aspects of life.

However, it is only fair to say that these human sins have been seen in all parts of the world and involve all types of peoples. To point this out is not to excuse it in any way, but to say that other major religious groups have also had and still have their own shameful and embarrassing history of the same type of evil system and treatment of minorities. Even today in a few countries some Arabs, including some nominal Christian Arabs, refer to a black person as "Abd" or "slave" in the Arabic language, even if he has never been a slave, but just because of his color. You can go to many places in East Africa (Kenya, Tanzania, and Zanzibar) where there are historical documents and even photos showing the involvement of black Africans capturing and selling their own neighboring tribesmen to the Arab slave traders who brought them with savage treatment in caravans to the coast for sale and/or transportation to other human markets throughout the world, including Arabia, Europe, and the Americas. The caves of Shimoni, Kenya, the holding prisons in Bagamoyo, Tanzania, and the slave markets of Zanzibar are still there as concrete historical reminders. Museums hold photos of people of all skin shades who were involved in this horrible crime. There are copies of original documents and photos of white-robed Arab merchants and white-skinned Europeans exchanging money for human lives, along with the chains and other weapons used for torture.

Numerous Christians, from Catholic priests and missionaries to the famous Protestant missionary, Dr. David Livingston, spurred other Europeans to work towards outlawing the institution of slave trade. Unfortunately, it took the Americans many more years and a civil war to outlaw the practice in our "one nation, under God," the United States. Yes, the United States is one nation *under God's judgment* for not living up to its Christian roots and teachings.

Even today, there are unofficial slaves in countries governed by supposedly "religious" principles. Allah in Christ would not condone the present mistreatment of servant women from the Philippines and elsewhere working in homes of the rich in Arabia or the sex-slaves brought from such countries as Romania and Mexico and abused in sinful, nominal Christian homes in Europe and America. Not only slaves and servants are discriminated against, but also some wives, even in front of their children, are harshly humiliated and beaten by their husbands with the permission of their religion (Sura 4:34). If the wife is much heavier and stronger, what happens if she feels unjustly beaten? Is she allowed to beat her much weaker husband when he makes such a miscalculated mistake? This discrimination against women is still allowed by religions in the Middle East, India, and many other parts of the world. It is even happening here in America, and sometimes with so-called Christians. Is there really any difference between racial discrimination and sexual discrimination? Whenever another human being is not treated with respect or with rights equal to another's, this is sin, no matter what type of religious faith or philosophy is being practiced and promoted by that society.

Jesus of Nazareth constantly taught and exemplified the great value of all women and men regardless of their outward characteristics, level of education, status in society, and religious or ethnic background. He related to and healed Jews and non-Jews alike, masters as well as servants, the religiously impure as well as those who were considered clean. The high value Christ placed on Gentiles went against the discrimination commonly practiced by His countrymen of that day. Just look at how He honored a Canaanite woman, probably a Palestinian who at that time were idol-worshipers, who cried for Him to heal her evil-possessed daughter. He gave His prejudiced disciples, who tried to send her away without being helped, an unforgettable lesson by praising her highly scrutinized faith in Him and healing her daughter (Matthew 15:21-28). We have already seen how He healed the servant of the Roman military officer and we know that the Romans were paganly worshiping their governmental leaders (Caesars). This love, respect, and healing action for these and others showed that Jesus Christ understood that there would be those from other religious backgrounds who would respond in faith to Him when they were given the good news concerning His authority and divine nature. They were not to be ignored, discriminated against, or forced to follow Him. They were to be lovingly included in the opportunities given to receive the security and privileges found only in God, the Father.

When, after His death and resurrection, Elohim's Moshiach, gave the great commission to His disciples that they should spread the good news about Him and His salvation, He made it plain that they should not keep it only for the Jews. He wanted to include the whole world in hearing His all-inclusive message. He said, "Go therefore and make disciples of *all* nations" (Matthew 28:19), and "You shall be my witnesses in Jerusalem and in all Judea and Samaria and to the *end of the earth*" (Acts 1: 8b). He knew that there was a universal hunger and thirst for the true God among adherents of all religions. He was repeating the ancient invitation: "Come, *all* you who are thirsty, come to the waters; and you who have no money, come, buy and eat!...Why spend money on what is not bread, and your labor on what does not satisfy?... Give ear and come to me; hear me, that your soul may live" (Isaiah 55:1-3).

Any form of discrimination or prejudice against God's created human beings is against Allah, Elohim, and is not His will. The basic solution for this is the same as for any other type of sin. We know that not only individuals, but whole families, communities, nations and even world systems can be in bondage to Satan, the enemy of God. This is seen in the prevalence of evil practices and inhuman treatment of others everywhere we look. What is the solution? Allah in Christ said, "If the Son sets you free, you will be free indeed" (John 8:36). To surrender one's will to the will of God in Christ will bring about a change in the heart, desires, attitudes, and actions of one person at a time, until more and more will come under the control of the powerful, loving God as they are freed from the destructive control of self and Satan. When we, *one person at a time*, have become children of God, rather than slaves of Satan, we will be able to follow God's teachings. "How great is the love the Father has lavished on us, that we should be called children of God!" (1 John. 3:1). "No one who is born of God will continue to sin, because God's seed remains in him, he cannot go on sinning, because he has been born of God. This is how we know who the children of God are and who the children of the devil are: Anyone who does not do what is right is not a child of God; nor is anyone who does not love his brother" (1 John. 3:9-10).

● ●

To Think about and Discuss

1. What are some examples of Jesus' own fair, non-prejudicial attitude toward others?

2. List some of the discriminatory attitudes and racial practices still in existence in our communities? In our nation?

3. Share a real situation in which you or someone else was discriminated against? How did that affect you or them?

4. What can you, personally, do in order to counteract attitudes and acts of discrimination and racism? Is this an important issue in the life of a believer in the true God? Why or why not?

PART VI

Elohim, Alahum: The Plural "One"

What Did Elohim's Moshiach, Allah's Masih, Jesus Christ, Claim about Himself?

*I*n almost every part of the world in which I've traveled and/or lived, I find the influence and benefits stemming from a man, Jesus Christ, who lived two thousand years ago. These influences are obvious in their calendars, their educational systems, the medical services being provided, the social programs for the poor and needy, the fight for the advancement of civil (including women's) rights and religious freedom, and in the governments where people are democratically represented. Yet, when talking to local citizens of any nation, many are completely unaware or have forgotten the source of these blessings, and some even deny and reject that they have received any benefits from this source.

Some people argue that while Jesus of Nazareth was a great teacher and a great moral man, He never claimed to be anything more than a human being. Anyone who has studied the sacred scriptures, the Bible, knows this is not true. In reading the Bible we realize that it was Jesus Himself who not only exhibited superhuman qualities, but also humbly and calmly made unusual claims about Himself. (Some of these claims are listed at the end of this chapter.) Drawing from the Old Testament prophecies, and in many different terms so that the slow to hear and believe could grasp the meaning, Jesus claimed that He came from God and was returning to God, that He was the Messiah, the Son of Man and the Son of God. He was persecuted, suffered and died upholding these claims. These claims are recorded for us in the New Testament gospels (Matthew, Mark, Luke, and John), and were written by or from the testimony of eye witnesses who had walked and talked with the Christ and observed first-hand His teachings and actions. The Bible (the Old and New Testaments) has been miraculously guarded and preserved in the original languages as well as in the translations through the centuries. The Quran, written in the Seventh Century A.D. accepted the Bible, affirmed Jews and Christians as "the people of the Book (Bible)," and related that God has promised to guard His word (Sura 10:94; 6:115). Although some people say that today's Bible has been changed from the Bible referred to in the Quran, this is not true. If the Bible was changed, where is the evidence? Where is that original Bible? Can't anyone find even one copy? No one has been able to find a single other or different Bible than the present one, that would confirm this charge. If the Bible had been changed, would the Jews have allowed the Christians to change the Old Testament? Would the Christians have allowed the Jews to change the New Testament, with the majority of its contents having been written during the lifetime of the first believers who were ear and eyewitnesses of Jesus' words and of the growth of the early church?

The controversial non-biblical "Gospel of Barnabas" (not to be confused with the Epistle of Barnabas, which is a completely different book), is quoted by some people to show the differences in its message from the biblical gospels (i.e. it claims that Jesus was not the Messiah and did not die on the cross, etc). This so-called "Barnabas Gospel" is completely unreliable, has been dated by scholars as originating from the sixteenth century (sixteen hundred years after the earthly life of Jesus Christ), and its message is completely refuted by the eyewitness accounts found in the New Testament dating from the first century.[19] It has never been accepted by any Christian group as being authentic.

"The book (the Bible), or the manuscripts, (which) the Quran referred to, existed hundreds of years before the birth of Islam's prophet. They still exist today so that any person may compare the text used today with the text of that day. There are complete Old and New Testament manuscripts written centuries before the Prophet of Islam, all of which are available today for inspection."[20] If there were a good, logical, and historically proven case that the Bible has been corrupted to change its message and meanings, every enemy of Christianity would be studying the Bible in order to find and point out its specific errors. If there were such a distortion, it could be easily demonstrated to all, including the Christian biblical scholars, by placing the original version alongside the present version and making it public knowledge for all to see. Yet, we find that those who disagree violently with the Bible's message are, in some countries, trying by all means to prevent its publication, distribution, or study by their own followers and even by the Christians living there. In fact, there is such a great fear that their people would read this Bible, that in some communist countries people are not even allowed to have a Bible in their possession! There would be no need to prohibit people from owning and reading a Bible if it could be proven to be false. "If it can be proven that the Holy Bible has been changed, then the Christian has no ground to stand upon. If, on the other hand, it has not been changed, and it is the true Word of Allah, then every person on earth should have an opportunity to (at least) read and understand it, for every human being on earth desires to have an encounter with the true and living Allah" [21]

Moslems understand that the Old and New Testaments were sent by God: "He (Allah) has revealed to you the Book with truth, verifying that which is before it, and He revealed the Torah and the Gospel aforetime, a guidance for the people …" (Sura 3:3), and "We sent after them in their footsteps Isa (Jesus), … verifying what was before him of the *Taurat* (Torah) and We gave him the *Injeel* (Gospel) in which was guidance and light" (Sura 5:46). They are assured that these written scriptures, the Old and New Testaments, will be protected and preserved by Allah so that mankind would not be misguided: "We have without doubt, sent the message; and We will assuredly guard it (from corruption)" (Sura 15:9). Furthermore in Sura 18:27 the Quran reaffirms that no one can change God's words. That should settle the question for Moslems who read the Quran that the Bible, as God's Word, has not been changed.

During the earthly lifetime of the Messiah, there were very few people beside Jesus' mother, Mary, and her betrothed husband, Joseph, to whom God directly revealed the supernatural (God/man) identity of Jesus (Isa) of Nazareth. They were told that the child would be the Savior, the presence of God with men (Immanuel), and the Son of God (Matthew 1:21, 22; Luke 1:35). The wise men/kings learned in a dream and came from the East to find the newborn king, the babe, Jesus Christ; brought Him gifts, and fell down and worshiped Him (Matthew 2:11). The prophet Yehya (John the Baptist) testified that he saw heaven open, saw the Spirit of God descend like a dove and alight on Jesus, and he heard God Himself speak from heaven claiming that Jesus Christ was His Son and the recipient of all the joy and blessings of the Father. "This is my beloved Son, with whom I am well pleased" (Matthew 3:16-17). When the man who had been born blind was healed by Jesus who later told him that He was the Son of Man (a title for the Messiah), the man believed and worshiped Him (John 9:35-38). Why would the truthful, ethical Jesus of Nazareth accept such worship if it was not true and if He were not worthy of men's worship?

The disciples who were with the Christ on a daily basis during His ministry took some time in trying to decide who He really was. They had asked each other upon Jesus' calming of the stormy sea, "Who then is this, that even wind and sea obey him?" (Mark 4:41b). When He asked them what other people believed about His identity, they answered, "Some say (you are) John the Baptist; others say Elijah; and still others, Jeremiah or one of the prophets." He said to them, "But who do you say I am?" Simon Peter replied, "You are the Christ (the Messiah), the Son of the living God" (Matthew 16:14-16). Did the honest and wise teacher, Jesus Christ, rebuke Peter for this blasphemy of attributing divine origin to a mere man? No, Jesus told Peter that he was blessed because God, not flesh and blood, had revealed this to him (Matthew 16:17). The disciple, Thomas, who had said he would not believe that the Christ had risen from the dead until he put his finger into the wounds of his hands and side, upon seeing these wounds, fell to Christ's feet in worship crying, "My Lord and my God!" (John 20:28). The Christ who was so zealous in correcting false concepts about the One, true God, did not correct Thomas when he gave to Him this title reserved for God alone In fact, Thomas's faith-filled reaction was a joy to the Messiah because when earlier before the crucifixion, when He was trying to prepare the disciples for his departure to the Father in heaven, Thomas had in doubt asked Him, "Lord we do not know where you are going, how can we know the way?" At that time the Christ had answered, "I am the way, and the truth, and the life; no one comes to the Father, but by me. If you had known me, you would have known my Father also; ... He who has seen me has seen the Father; how can you say, 'Show us the Father'? Do you not believe that I am in the Father and the Father in me?" (John 14:6, 7).

How surprising to note that the evil spirits which Jesus drove out of people were very much aware of His divine identity. They cried out in respect and fear because they knew of His power over them. Some of their cries were: "What have you to do with us, O Son of God: Have you come here to torment us before the time?" (Matthew 8:29), "What have you to do with us, Jesus of Nazareth? Have you come to destroy us? I know who you are, the Holy One of God" (Mark. 1:24), and "You are the Son of God!" (Luke 4:41).

Jesus Christ did not dispute the testimony of the evil spirits, He accepted people's *worship* of Him (Mark 5:6, John 9:38, Matthew 8:2, 9:18, 15:25, and 20:20), and also made the mind-staggering claim that He, the Son of God, is to be honored as well as God the Father. He said, "The Father judges no one but has given all judgment to the Son, that all may honor the Son, even as they honor the Father. He who does not honor the Son does not honor the Father who sent him" (John 5:22-23). Jesus is the final Judge for all men. In addition to the Christians who are preparing for Christ's

> ## The Judge is coming – ready or not!

return (Matthew 16:27), even Moslems are now waiting for Him as the Judge, and many Jews are still expecting the coming of their Messiah. In fact, *Jesus Christ* is the only person who will fulfill the expectations of all three groups (Jews, Moslems, and Christians) who are expectantly awaiting His coming/return to earth.

The last words Jesus uttered while being crucified on the cross were: "It is *finished*" (John 19:30). By these words He was claiming that by His sacrificial suffering and death – God's plan of salvation – had been completed. There would be no need for another sacrifice, prophet, or revelation from God that would change or add to this completed work on the cross. Therefore, dear reader, we are left with a personal choice. Either these claims of the Christ are true and we recognize Him as God in the flesh; or He was a liar and fraud, or at least a madman with delusions of greatness. Which choice fits best with what Allah al-Hakim (God, the Wise) is revealing to you? This is the most important choice we will ever make because our choice will make the difference between our eternal life or our eternal death. For "there is salvation in no one else, for there is no other name (Jesus Christ) under heaven given among men by which we must be saved" (Acts 4:12). Just as we each must enter heaven or hell alone, every person must choose alone. It is not a matter of blind conformity to the majority or to the religious leadership of our family, community, church, synagogue, or mosque. You and I are responsible to choose our own destiny based on the light God gives us. As the Messiah taught, "Enter by the narrow gate; for the gate is wide and the way is easy, that leads to destruction, and those who enter by it are many. For the gate is narrow and the way is hard, that leads to life, and those who find it are few" (Matthew 7:13-14).

Thank God that after we have made our individual decisions and have entered in through the narrow gate, we are no longer alone. We are filled with God's own Spirit who will stick with us closer than a brother, sister, father, son or any earthly friend because of our having chosen Jesus Christ as our Savior and Lord. We will find wonderful daily fellowship in the presence of God, and He will bring us into fellowship with other believers in the Body of Christ, known as the church.

Claims Made by
Jesus Christ, Isa, the Messiah

Reference	Claim
Matthew 9:6	- to be able to forgive sins
Matthew 11:27	- to reveal God to men
Matthew 11:28-29	- to give rest and comfort to the weary and troubled
Matthew 16:27; 24:30	- to be coming again to earth in the glory of the Father with His angels
Matthew 26:28	- that His shed blood would provide forgiveness of sins for those who believe
Matthew 26:64	- to share the heavenly throne with God in the future in heaven
Matthew 28:18	- to have been given all authority in heaven and earth
Mark 2:28	- to be the Master of the Sabbath (the holy day of worship)
Mark 10:45	- to give His life as a ransom (payment to deliver one from captivity) for others
John 2:19-22	- to raise Himself three days after death
John 3:36; 4:10,14; 5:24; 11:25	- to be able to give people eternal life
John 5:17-18	- to be equal with God
John 5:21	- to give life to the dead
John 5:26	- to be equal with God in His immortality
John 6:35	- to be the bread of life

John 7:37	- to be the water of life
John 8:12	- to be the light of the world
John 8:58	- to have existed eternally before Abraham was born, and will continue to exist forever
John 10:7, 9	- to be the door to salvation
John 10:10	- to have come to give men life
John 10:11	- to be the good shepherd who lays down His life for the sheep
John 10:18	- to have control over the timing and manner of His own death
John 10:30	- to be one with the Father
John 10:37-38	- to be in the Father and the Father in Him as proved by His miracles
John 12:32	- to be able to draw all men to Him through His sacrifice on the cross
John 12:45	- to be the visible form of the invisible God
John 13:13	- to be the Lord and Master
John 14:6	- to be the only way to God; the only truth and life
John 15:24	- to have done works no other man had done
John 16:15	- to have all of God's wisdom at His disposal to be revealed to His followers by the Holy Spirit
John 17:5	- to have been present in a glorious state with God before the world was created
Revelation 1:8, 17	- to be the Alpha and Omega, the First and the Last

To Think about and Discuss

1. Is there anything Jesus said or did that can convince you that He was a mere man or just a good prophet?

2. Go through each of Jesus' unique claims about Himself as listed in the chart at the end of this chapter and read each biblical reference. Compare these claims with those made by the Old Testament prophets and the prophet of Islam.

3. Which of these claims of Jesus are easy for you to believe? Why? Which are difficult to believe? Why?

4. What difference will it make to you if these claims are true? If they are false?

Elohim, Allah, God in Christ: The Second Person of the Trinity?

*D*ear Reader, it has been fifty years since I was personally confronted with the claims of Christ and had to try to honestly answer some tough questions. I am, hereby, challenging you to also do the same. Ask yourself the following questions and please, for your own sake, answer honestly: YES or NO.

— Was Jesus (Isa) of Nazareth more than an ordinary religious man or prophet?
— Was He the anointed one (the Messiah, the Christ), appointed to do a special task for God?
— Was He a wonderful, wise, miracle-working, kind, and perfect example of the God who sent Him to earth?
— When you hear Jesus' words, do you recognize that Elohim, Allah, God, is speaking to you?
— When you see His actions and motives of love and compassion for men, do you believe that He acted in just the same way that God would act in the same situation?

— When the Christ impresses you with your need to repent of your sins and accept His sacrifice for you on the cross, do you find your heart desiring to do so?

If you have answered *yes*, would that be blasphemy on your part? Wouldn't you be considered an infidel or kafir? "Yes, this would be blasphemy if Christ is only a mere human being, but it would be the only reasonable response, if He is divine." But how could He be divine (have the nature of God)? Wouldn't that make two Gods: Christ and Elohim/Allah Akbar? No!

How contradictory – to question the Almighty's plan!

We have been explaining in this book how the only true God, Elohim Kabeer, Allah Akbar sent the Christ and was in the Christ. Is this confusing? Can God be the one and only Divinity in the universe and still have a unity of richness and fullness of personality in the nature of His very being? Yes, Allah who is Akbar in His nature, can be whatever He has designed! If God is God, He can be whatever His nature demands, without any input, advice, or need for satisfying our logic! The Almighty has His secrets, including the mystery surrounding the fullness of His own incomprehensible nature; and He makes His own decisions about which of these secrets He will reveal to men, and at what time and in what manner. "The secret things belong to the Lord our God, but the things revealed belong to us and to our children forever" (Deuteronomy 29:29). Our role is not to question His secrets, but to accept and give thanks for His revelations that are given to us.

In the Hebrew Scriptures the word which was used for the

one true God was sometimes used in the singular *El* or *Eloah*, (*Ilah* in Arabic) and many times (actually more than two thousand times) in the plural *Elohim*. For example, while the first verse in the Torah says, "In the beginning God created the heavens and the earth" (Genesis 1:1), verse twenty-six of the same chapter says, "Then God said, 'Let *us* make man in *our* image, after *our* likeness" (Genesis 1:26). This happens other times in Scripture as well, for example, in Genesis 18 where God is described as *one* and as *three* persons at the same time. Even in the Quran, the Arabic language plural form *Allahum* from the singular Allah (which is similar to the plural Hebrew form *Elohim*) was used to refer to the *one* God, Allah. Also in many suras of the Quran when Allah is quoted, He refers to Himself as *we* and *our*.

Christians have tried to put into words the nature of the one God as found in the entire Bible, both the Old and New Testaments. They noted that the one God who had been worshiped by the Jews for centuries has three centers of personality: the Father, the Son, and the Holy Spirit, which express a rich unity of relationship and purpose. The Apostle Paul had tried to explain it by saying that there is no God but *one* (1 Corinthians 8:4); yet he clearly declared that the mystery of Godliness is great: "He (God) was manifested in the flesh (in Jesus Christ), (and) vindicated in the Spirit" (1 Timothy 3:16). Paul was a Jewish religious scholar entrenched in the truth of the Oneness of God and was a persecutor of Christians, but when the crucified and risen Jesus Christ appeared to him on the road to Damascus, he came to believe that Jesus Christ was also God (Acts 9:3-30). It took God, Himself, to remove the cloud of historical Judaism's limited interpretations from Paul's eyes and the doubt from his mind in such an indisputable way that he spent the rest of his life explaining this "mystery of Godliness" to other Jews and to Gentiles as well. He became very convinced that no one can deny Elohim the right and the power to incarnate Himself in the body that He prepared here on earth for Jesus Christ. In fact, this was the fulfillment of King David's prophecy that the Messiah would say: "Sacrifice and offering you did not desire, but a body you (the Father) prepared for me" (Hebrews 10:5).

Paul and the disciples remembered the teachings of Jesus that He would send the Holy Spirit who had always been present and active in the Old Testament, in a new and powerful way (Acts1:4-5, 8). The coming of this personal life-changing Spirit, which had been predicted by the prophets (Isaiah 32:15; Ezek. 36:26-27; Joel 2:28-29), happened at Pentecost (Acts 2:1-21). At that time, when the believers in Christ actually experienced clearly the Spirit's presence and power in their lives, they knew that the Holy Spirit was not only proceeding from God, but also, was God. They discovered the truth of Christ's words that the Holy Spirit would live with and in the believer as an eternal Counselor to reveal the truth, to teach them from the Father and from the Son all the things that they would need to know, and would be their companion and guide (John. 13:16-17, 26; John 16:7, 12-15). They found Jesus' promise to be true, that it would be the Spirit who would work to convict the sinner of his guilt and convince him that the solution was to be found in the sinless Savior who had defeated Satan on the cross (John 16:8-11). Jesus' followers came to depend on the Holy Spirit whom they experienced, not as a mere power, but as the very person and character of God!

This was such a new and unique concept: that the core of the One True God's very nature, not just His functioning, could be so varied, rich, and full! It took some time before the early church leaders could put into a few concise words what the disciples and other eyewitnesses had seen, heard, and experienced. They lived with the expanded yet obvious revelation of God given in the person of Jesus Christ, and in the working of the Holy Spirit in the early church. This caused some of them to return to the Old Testament to search out again the root revelations and beginning descriptions of God's triune nature starting even with the first verses of the first chapter of the first books of the Old and New Testaments. "In the beginning God created the heavens and the earth. Now the earth was formless and empty, darkness was over the surface of the deep, and the Spirit of God was hovering over the waters" (Genesis 1:1, 2). "Then God said, 'Let *us* make man in *our* image, in *our* likeness...'" (Genesis 1:26). "In the beginning was the Word, and the Word was with God, and the Word was God. He was with God in the beginning. Through him all things were made... The Word became flesh and made his dwelling among us. We have seen his glory, the glory of the one and only, who came from the Father, full of grace and truth" (John. 1:1-3a, 14).

As in most languages, the word "one" can mean a singular subject such as in "one man," and it can mean a subject composed of compound parts such as "one flesh," the term used by God to describe marriage as the union of one man and one woman as noted in Genesis 2:24, or "one day" which was composed of the morning and the evening as noted in Genesis 1:5. The Hebrew word for one *'ehadh* used in these two examples meant "one from compounded parts;" the other word for one *yahadh* which means "absolute indivisible unity or oneness" was not used. We note that the Hebrew word *'ehadh* is also used to describe the Oneness of God in Deuteronomy 6:4: "Jehovah our God (*Elohim*) is one (*'ehadh*) Jehovah." [23] God's very first two commandments – "You shall have no other gods before me" and "You shall not make for yourself an idol" – (Exodus 20:3-6) demanded strict monotheism and commanded severe punishment for any transgressor, yet, the word yahadh (absolute indivisible unity) is not used here in Deuteronomy 6:4 to describe the oneness of God. It is not just an accident that the word for God (*Elohim*) is in the plural and the word for one (*'ehadh*) is in the compound meaning.

The outcome of the study and the consultation of Christians as they grappled with this subject in the early centuries after Christ's ascension to heaven led to the official historical recognition that came to be known as the doctrine of the Trinity: The Father is God, the Son is God, the Holy Spirit is God, and *these three together are the One Triune God.* Just as the Moslem word "Tawheed" (which describes the doctrine of Oneness of God) is not found in the Quran, so also the Christian word "Trinity" (which describes the doctrine of the triune nature of the One God) is not found in the Bible. The concept of Tawheed is based on the teachings of the Quran not on the word "Tawheed;" and the concept of the Trinity is based on teachings found throughout the Bible, but not on the word "Trinity."

It must be noted that by describing the nature of God as a Trinity, Christians are not saying that there are three Gods. No! God forbid! They are saying that the Bible in its entirety (Old and New Testaments combined) has recorded how God revealed Himself, how He has acted in the world, and how He interacted with men throughout history. This same Bible teaches that the Father is God, the Son is God, and the Holy Spirit is God and that these three together are the *one* and *only* True God! After examining the revelation we have been given in the written Word of God — the Bible, — and in the Living Word of God — Jesus Christ; and in our experience with the indwelling Holy Spirit — there is no other conclusion to be drawn.

Some Christian scientists, who also have been observing the truth about God from studying the natural world which He has created, have come to the same conclusion: that His nature is triune. They believe that not only from studying the Bible, but also by observing the results of His creation, it is possible to find evidence of the nature and characteristics of His divine being. For example, by studying the objects of His creative activity, we learn that He is not only powerful, but purposeful, as He brought the light out of darkness and set up the heavenly bodies with the objective of providing the only perfect environment in the universe where it is possible for man to live and to meet his needs. In His creation of man and interaction with Him in time and history, we see that God is a relational Being who desires to be involved personally in the lives of men as individuals and people groups.

Scientists, not only theologians, have found examples in the organization and function of the natural world that have led them to recognize how God's divine nature could be understood as three-dimensional. As explained by Dr. James Kennedy, the complex concept of *time*, which was created by God, is in some ways an analogy for the concept of the Trinity.[22] The concept of Time is made up of three parts: the future, the present, and the past which can perhaps help us to understand the concept that God can be both *one* and a *unity* made up of the Father, the Son, and the Holy Spirit. This is not foreign to us as we already understand that God is eternal and remains the same yesterday and today and forever (Hebrews 13:8). Therefore, in our attempt to understand how God can be "three in one" as time can be "three in one," let us only for purposes of illustration exchange in our minds the concept of the future with the concept of the Father, exchange the concept of the present with the concept of the Son, and exchange the concept of the past with the concept of the Holy Spirit. Then let us continue to consider that just like God the Father, the future is unseen and unknown, but continually embodies itself or makes itself known and visible in the present (just as God, the Father did in the Son). The present is what we experience for a limited time just as Christ's life on earth was limited. We can clearly see, hear, and know the present as it always brings into today's concrete reality what the invisible future has in store. The Son, Jesus Christ is what has been seen, heard, and known in the fullness of His life and death as He embodied the invisible Father in His (Christ's) day-by-day, hour-by-hour, and moment-by-moment earthly existence. Just as the present has always existed as long as time has existed, so the Son has always existed and will always exist just as God has and always will exist. It is through the present (or the Son in our metaphor), that the future (or the Father) becomes a concrete reality in human experience. The past (or in our analogy, the Holy Spirit) comes from the present and the future without embodying the present; that is, the past is invisible and proceeds silently and continuously from the visible present and the invisible future. In the same manner, the Holy Spirit who was from the beginning of creation with God (Genesis 1:2) was sent through the Son from the Father without having a body like the Son does. After the Son of God (Jesus Christ) left this earth and ascended to heaven, the invisible Holy Spirit continually casts light upon the Son by helping us understand His teachings and giving testimony about His nature, just like the past casts light upon the present. We are able to understand the present and have confidence in the future because of what the past reveals to us. The Holy Spirit helps us to recognize the Son, with whom we live in daily relationship, and to recognize the Father, whom we expect to see face to face in the future. In Heaven, the mystery of the One Triune God will be fully revealed and that overwhelming

$$1 \times 1 \times 1 = 1$$

reality of God Almighty will cause us, along with peoples from every tribe and nation, to fall to our knees in praise and thanksgiving! (Revelation 7:9-12).

This analogy of the Trinity can be symbolized in mathematical language as:

FUTURE X PRESENT X PAST = TIME.

This is an exact mathematical analogy of:

FATHER X SON X HOLY SPIRIT = GOD.

This is similar to the unique concept of multiplying "three ones" in mathematics: $1 \times 1 \times 1 = 1$, where the result is still one; we have ONE God. The mathematical results between multiplication and addition are clearly distinct. With the nature of God, we do not use addition which is simply $1 + 1 + 1 = 3$. We do not have three Gods!

The Bible teaches that the purpose behind God's special revelation of His rich, full, divine nature to be Three in One was so that people like you and me in all times of history could better understand Him and come to love and experience Him in His Fullness!

There is no reason to fear this Glorious God and His will for you. He has said that "whoever comes to me, I will never cast out" (John. 6:37), *He* is the one who has the keys to heaven through *His* solution. You can depend on *His* salvation, not on the amount of your good works and acts of worship. Only when we accept Christ's blood for our salvation, replacing all the blood of sheep sacrifices or other good acts, can we respond correctly and live in repentance, faith, gratitude, praise, worship, and service. We will bring glory to God when we submit (true Tasleem) our changed lives to live daily under His direction and in His presence. This daily invisible presence of God the Holy Spirit in Christ, promises that He will never leave us alone: "I am with you always, even to the end of the world" (Matthew 28:20b). God's Spirit will provide us the peace, counsel, correction, and guidance needed to meet the problems and temptations which life on this earth will continue to bring our way. We trust in the promise that "God is faithful and He will not let you be tempted beyond your strength, but with the temptation will also provide the way of escape, that you may be able to endure it" (1 Corinthians 10:13). There is no adequate way to describe the joy, even midst life's problems, that the believer in Christ experiences as he lives with the daily assurance that he is accepted by the Only True God because of what was done for him on the cross. What a relief to know that our salvation does not depend on the amounts of money we give to the poor or for construction of worship buildings, or on the amount of time we spend in fasting or prayer; but on the grace of God who loves us and who works all things for the good of those who will accept Him as their Father and Savior. After we have accepted His sacrifice for us, He will lead us into the ways He wants to communicate with us through reading His Word, how we can communicate with Him through prayer, and how to please Him by helping our neighbors and even our enemies. These actions are a result and proof of our salvation, not a means to earn it.

Ask Elohim, Allah, from your heart if He is really your Father, if He is truly in Christ, and if He (by His Spirit) is willing to live in close communion with you daily. You will get the answer! If you are sincerely open to His will and are putting aside any pre-conceived ideas and decisions, He will reveal the truth to you, and guarantee to you a new quality of life which will be everlasting. Your decision to receive this new life is not a choice of your intellect about which doctrine sounds most logical or suits your background best, but a decision of your will to follow His truth. Just how strong is your desire to live in close communion with God? Are you like the Psalmist who cried out to God, "As the deer pants for streams of water, so my soul pants for you, O God. My soul thirsts for God, for the living God. When can I go and meet with God?" (Psalm 42: 1-2). If you are longing for the peace that comes from knowing that when you die you are assured by God of salvation, listen to these words: "If you confess with your lips that Jesus is Lord, and believe in your heart that God raised Him from the dead, you will be saved" (Romans 10:9). Act now, there is no need to wait in dread until the Judgment Day for your good and evil acts to be examined and weighed. Jesus assured us that it is not the will of God the Father that any of His children would perish (Matthew 18:14). Say, "Yes!" to Elohim, Allah, as He reveals Himself in the Father, the Son, and the Holy Spirit. He will assure you that He is with you until the end of the world. We can depend on the Great God, who in Christ promised His followers that "in this world you will have trouble. But take heart! I have overcome the world" (John 16:33b).

• •

To Think about and Discuss

1. Examine Chapter 18 of Genesis and see how God revealed Himself to Abraham as one and three at the same time.

2. Search the Old Testament for the references to or indications of the Holy Spirit and the Son of God and/or Son of Man.

3. Note in these scriptures (John 14:16-17, 25-26, 16:7-15, and Acts 3:3-4) how Jesus and the apostles refer to the Holy Spirit as "He" (a personality) and not "it" (like an object or impersonal force).

4. Human beings are very limited in our ability to comprehend the things of God, especially His own nature. Can this be the reason why one of His Spirit's main functions is to explain and reveal to men such mysteries as the Incarnation of Christ and the "Three in One" nature of God?

Christ: Creator and Re-Creator?

*F*or by him (Christ) all things *were created*: things in heaven and on earth, visible and invisible, ... all things were created by him and for him. He is before all things, and in him all things hold together"
(Colossians 1:16-17).

"Therefore, if anyone is in Christ, he is a *new creation*; the old has gone, the new has come!
(2 Corinthians 5:17).

Christ said to the Jewish leaders, "Before Abraham was born, I am!" (John 8:58). The Jews knew that the only other One to have ever used this term or name, *"I am,"* was Elohim Kabeer, Almighty God. When Moses had asked His name, God had replied, *"I am who I am"* (Exodus 3:14), which means: I have always been God, I am God now, and I will always be God in the future! Paul also testified about Christ's eternal nature when he spoke about His role in creation: "For by him (Christ) all things were created: things in heaven and on earth, visible and invisible, whether thrones or powers or rulers or authorities; all things were created by him and for him. He is before all things, and in him all things hold together... For God was pleased to have all his fullness dwell in him (Christ)... making peace through his blood, shed on the cross" (Colossians 1:16-17, 19-20).

When the Triune God created Adam from the earth, he was not organically different from animals, but God breathed into him His Spirit and Adam became also a spiritual being. He, like animals had flesh, blood, and bones, but was different in several ways including having the free will to worship and obey God or to do the opposite. When Adam and Eve obeyed Satan rather than God, they deserved God's wrath and were kicked out of the garden of Eden. Adam and his descendents could not save themselves even though they tried by their worship, offerings, and good works. Therefore God sent His eternally existing Son, to become flesh in the person of Jesus of Nazareth. Jesus, the second type of Adam, corrected what the first Adam had distorted. Whereas the first Adam brought sin upon all men and its penalty of death, the second brought the gift of righteousness and life. "But the gift is not like the trespass. For if the many died by the trespass of the one man (Adam), how much more did God's grace and the gift that came by the grace of the one man, Jesus Christ, overflow to the many! (Romans 5:15). Since the time of His giving on the cross that gift of life, Christ the Creator of life has become the Re-Creator of life.

The pinnacle of power: creation and re-creation!

The Quran seems to agree with this concept that the Creator who raised up the first man, Adam, out of the lifeless clay to become a living being, is the only One able to recreate His creation, raising them up from death to eternal life! Al-Ba'ith (the Resurrector) is one of the ninety-nine names given God by the Quran and it signifies God's power of resurrecting someone whom He had originally created. The teaching is that the first creation of the world by Allah is proof that He is able to continue creating. "The one who will resurrect us will be the one who first made us (Sura 17:50). This interpretation of a second creation as part of the resurrection is defended by Al-Ghazili. 'The resurrection refers to bringing the dead to life by creating them once more.'" [24]

God, in Christ has been spiritually re-creating the hundreds of millions of lives of those who, one by one, accept His sacrificial love for them. For, "If anyone is in Christ, he is a new creation; the old has gone, the new has come. All this is from God who reconciled us to himself through Christ" (2 Corinthians 5:17-18). If you accept this gift given not just for others, but for you personally by name, you are guaranteed a new life here and now that will also continue for eternity in that place He has prepared and is awaiting you in heaven. Whether you have been aware of this good news all your life as a nominal Christian, or if you are from another background and this is the first time you have heard, the Spirit of God is able to make this truth clearly irresistible as it fulfills your heart's desires. God in Christ will be your companion forever, for He promised: "Surely I am with you always, to the end of the age" (Matthew 28:20).

The Incomparable Christ

*M*ore than nineteen hundred years ago, there was a Man who lived in poverty and was reared in obscurity. He possessed neither wealth nor influence. In infancy He startled a king; in childhood He puzzled doctors; in manhood He ruled the course of nature, walked upon the waves as if they were pavements, and hushed the sea to sleep. He used no medicines and yet He healed multitudes. He never wrote a book, and yet all the libraries of the country could not hold the books that have been written about Him. He never wrote a song, and yet He has furnished the theme for more songs than all the songwriters combined. He never marshaled an army, nor drafted a soldier, nor fired a gun; and yet no leader ever had more volunteers who have, under His orders, persuaded more rebels to stack arms and surrender without a shot fired. Every seventh day the wheels of commerce cease their turning, and multitudes wind their way to worshiping assemblies to pay homage and respect to Him. The names of the past scientists, philosophers, and theologians have come and gone; but the Name of this Man abounds more and more. Though time has spread nineteen hundred years between the people of this generation and the scene of His crucifixion, He still lives. Herod could not destroy Him, and the grave could not hold Him. He stands forth upon the highest pinnacle of glory, proclaimed of God, acknowledged by angels, adored by saints, and feared by devils, as the living Personal Christ, our Lord and Savior!

Author Unknown

Footnotes

[1] John Esposito, ed., *The Oxford Encyclopedia of the Islamic World*, Vol. 1 (New York: Oxford University Press, 1995), 76.

[2] ____ *The Aramaic New Covenant*, A Literal Translation & Transliteration by Herb Jahn, Exegete, (Orange, Calif.: Exegesis Bibles, 1996), 85a.

[3] David B. Barrett, George T. Kurian, and Todd M. Johnson, eds. *World Christian Encyclopedia*, Vol. 2 (New York: Oxford University Press, 2001), 252.

[4] Ibid., 254.

[5] W. E. Vine, Merrill F. Unger, and William White, Jr., *Vine's Complete Expository of Old and New Testament Words* (Nashville: Thomas Nelson Publishers, 1996), Old Testament Section, 96.

[6] Patrick Johnstone and Jason Mandryk, *Operation World*, 21st Century Edition (Bulstrode, U.K.: WEC International, 2001), 557.

[7] William J. Saal, *Reaching Muslims for Christ* (Chicago: Moody Press, 1993), 33.

[8] Norman L. Geisler and Abdul Saleeb, *Answering Islam* (Grand Rapids: Baker Books, 1993), 13-14.

[9] Samuel M. Zwemer, *The Moslem Doctrine of God* (American Tract Society, 1905), 25.

[10] John S. Mbiti, *Concepts of God in Africa* (London: S.P.C.K., 1970), 179.

[11] Ibid., 194.

[12] Don Richardson, *Eternity in Their Hearts* (Ventura, Calif.: Regal Books, 1981), 44

[13] Hayin Baltsan, *Websters' New World Hebrew Dictionary, Hebrew English - English Hebrew Transliterated Dictionary* (Cleveland: Wiley Publishing, Inc., 1992), 598.

[14] Mark Eastman, M.D. and Chuck Smith, *The Search for the Messiah* (Fountain Valley, Calif.: Joy Publishing, 1996), 225.

[15] Geisler and Saleeb, 22-25.

[16] Vine, Op. Cit., New Testament Section, 1.

[17] Johnstone and Mandryk, Op. Cit., 362.

[18] Ibid., 13-14.

[19] Geisler and Saleeb, 296-298.

[20] Del Kingsriter, *Muslims & Christians Journey to Understanding* (Minneapolis: Center for Ministry to Muslims, 1987), 14.

[21] Ibid.

[22] D. James Kennedy, "The Trinity All Around You" (unpublished manuscript, drawing from material from Dr. Nathan R. Wood's book, *The Secret of the Universe*.)

[23] Lewis Sperry Chafer, *Systematic Theology*, Vol.1 (Dallas: Dallas Seminary Press, 1947), 266-7.

[24] David Bentley, *The 99 Beautiful Names of God* (Pasadena, Calif.: William Carey Library, 1999), 49.

Bibliography

_____ *The Aramaic New Covenant.* (A Literal Translation & Transliteration by Herb Jahn, Exegete). Orange, Calif.: Exeges's Bibles, 1996.

_____ *Al Quran Al Kareem.* (In the Arabic language)

Baltsan, Hayin. *Websters' New World Hebrew Dictionary, Hebrew English - English Hebrew Transliterated Dictionary.* Cleveland: Wiley Publishing, Inc., 1992.

Barrett, David B., George T. Kurian, and Todd M. Johnson, eds. *World Christian Encyclopedia,* Vol. 2. New York: Oxford University Press, 2001.

Bentley, David. *The 99 Beautiful Names of God.* Pasadena, Calif.: William Carey Library, 1999.

Chafer, Lewis Sperry. *Systematic Theology,* Vol. I. Dallas: Dallas Seminary Press, 1947.

Eastman, Mark, M.D. and Chuck Smith. *The Search for the Messiah.* Fountain View, Calif.: Joy Publishing, 1996.

Exposito, John, ed. *The Oxford Encyclopedia of the Modern Islamic World.* New York: Oxford University Press, 1995.

Geisler, Norman L. and Abdul Saleeb. *Answering Islam: The Crescent in the Light of the Cross.* Grand Rapids: Baker Books, 1993.

_____ *The Holy Bible.* (Verses quoted from the Revised Standard Version and the New International Version except where otherwise indicated).

Johnstone, Patrick, and Jason Mandryk. *Operation World,* 21st Century Edition. Bulstrode, U.K.: WEC International, 2001.

Kateregga, Badru D., and David W. Shenk. *Islam and Christianity.* Nairobi: Uzima Press Ltd., 1980.

Kennedy, D. James. "The Trinity All Around You," *unpublished manuscript*. Ft. Lauderdale, Fla., 2004.

Kingsriter, Del. *Muslims & Christians Journey to Understanding*. Minneapolis, Minn.: Center for Ministry to Muslims, 1987.

Mbiti, John. *Concepts of God in Africa*. London: S.P.C.K., 1970.

Parshall, Phil. *New Paths in Muslim Evangelism*. Grand Rapids: Baker Books, 1980.

_____ *The Qur'an*. (English Translation by M. H. Shakir). Elmhurst, N.Y.: Tahrike Tarsile Qur'an, Inc., 2002.

Rhodes, Ron. *Reasoning from the Scriptures with Muslims*. Eugene, Ore.: Harvest House Publishers, 2002.

Richardson, Don. *Eternity in Their Hearts*. Ventura, Calif.: Regal Books, 1981.

Saal, William J. *Reaching Muslims for Christ*. Chicago: Moody Press, 1993.

Vine, W. E., Merrill F. Unger, and William White, Jr. *Vine's Complete Expository Dictionary of Old and New Testament Words*. Nashville: Thomas Nelson Publishers, 1996.

Wooten, RWF, ed. *Jesus - More Than a Prophet*. Bromley: Inter-Varsity Press, 1982.

Zwemer, Samuel. *The Moslem Doctrine of God*. American Tract Society, 1905.